T0082776

The Rubber Tapper's Son

The Rubber Tapper's Son

Apparow Sannasai PhD

PARTRIDGE

Copyright © 2017 by Apparow Sannasai PhD.

ISBN: Softcover   978-1-5437-4213-8
           eBook   978-1-5437-4214-5

All rights reserved. No part of this book may be used or reproduced by any means, graphic, electronic, or mechanical, including photocopying, recording, taping or by any information storage retrieval system without the written permission of the author except in the case of brief quotations embodied in critical articles and reviews.

Because of the dynamic nature of the Internet, any web addresses or links contained in this book may have changed since publication and may no longer be valid. The views expressed in this work are solely those of the author and do not necessarily reflect the views of the publisher, and the publisher hereby disclaims any responsibility for them.

Print information available on the last page.

To order additional copies of this book, contact
Toll Free 800 101 2657 (Singapore)
Toll Free 1 800 81 7340 (Malaysia)
orders.singapore@partridgepublishing.com

www.partridgepublishing.com/singapore

Dedicated to my Family Members:

Past
Father: Sannasai Paidiah
Mother: Letchumanah Selliah
Younger Brother: Subramaniam Sannasai

AND

Present
Wife: Ramaluamah Maraniah
Daughter: Nishanthi Apparow
Son: Sanjeeva Rao Apparow
Elder Brother: Krishnan Sannasai & Family
Elder Sister: Ramulamah Sannasai & Family

Contents

Toddler days and the joyous childhood

Many Hindus in Malaysia pay homage to Lord Muruga at Batu Caves, Kuala Lumpur on Thaipusam day every year once. Thaipusam is a Hindu festival and is an auspicious day for the Hindus. It is celebrated grandly by the Malaysian Hindus in Malaysia.

In the zodiac when the circumventing moon touches upon the star of 'Pusam' the festival Thaipusam is celebrated. The atmosphere is usually big and it is filled with devotional songs. The devotees of Lord Muruga from all over Malaysia and other parts of the world come in bus loads to pay homage to their deity Lord Muruga on this holy day.

It seems I got lost in the Thaipusam crowd at the Batu Caves Festival when I was about three years old. In that big crowd I must have drifted away from my parents. My parents and relatives were looking for me frantically. My father scolded my mother for neglecting me. She however was already burdened attending to my sister and brother who are only a few years older than me. My younger brother was not born then.

My parents despair was short lived. They found relieve when the Temple public announcement system brought in to their attention the sound of a wailing child crying for his mother. The announcers managed to extract my name and they dutifully announced to the crowd of a toddler being lost. Fortunately, my uncle who was also there at the Batu Caves recognized my wailing voice. He approached the Public Announcement (PA) system office to rescue me as my guardian angel. By then both my parents have also heard my crying voice and they too came to the PA system office.

Despair turned to happiness upon the reunion of their son joining them back. I must have been oblivion to what was happening but after seeing my mother again all the fears and apprehensions disappeared. Joining back to the family fold was the best security for a three year old toddler.

I could not remember any part of the incident. When I grew big, my mother broke the news of my misadventure. I read that Jesus Christ too got lost at the Jerusalem temple when he was about twelve years old. His parent's were also frantically searching for him. Later they found him in the midst of the temple priests inquiring on the various issues of the temple.

I associated myself with Jesus Christ and was comparing myself with him. I was dreaming then that I too could turn out to be as popular as Jesus Christ when I grow up. On retrospect I am amused as to how on earth I could compare myself with Jesus Christ. Whenever I think of this thought, I feel shy at the stupidity and simplicity of a teenager. Anyway it was just a silly thought that was being entertained by an immature mind. I suppose most youths would have had these types of imaginations or fantasies.

As a child, my life was very joyous. I had no other work except to play and be care free. Food was ever ready for lunch and dinner. Food was never an issue and hunger was a very rare experience. I was fortunate for food was always available in the kitchen. In addition to these, mother would always have some tit-bits bottled up for us to eat at any time of our choice.

I remember the childhood days vividly. Deepavali days were joyous occasions for us. We got new dresses and shoes. I still remember at one Deepavali day I was sporting white socks and white shoes. Those shoes also doubled up as shoes which we wear for school. I wore the socks until knee height and was parading my new white socks to my fellow friends. They too paraded their new clothes and most of us were oblivion of other things. For us to show our new attire were our pride for the day.

We were very happy indeed that we got to wear a new shirt and new pants. To us that is an indication to us that our parents loved us. Parents do know that we kids do compare our attires and they make sure to buy for us the best for their respective children. It was their Deepavali present for their children. Anything less will make the child sad and most parents do not want to see their children disappointed.

We become joyous after receiving some goodies from the estate planter's wife. It was a norm in my rubber estate that the manager's or rather the planter's wife would distribute goodies to the workers children on that day. We were made to line up and receive the goodies from the Ma'am (wife of the planter) as a gesture of appreciation to the estate workers by the estate management for Deepavali celebrations. We get fruits such as oranges and apples. We are also loaded with western chocolates and biscuits which were rare goodies for us then.

Life was indeed a pleasure. Being care free was the practice of the days. Sometimes in the early part of the months there will be an open-air cinema shows. Popular Tamil film shows would be shown. These cinema shows were self sponsored by the estate workers money. To them viewing the films in this manner were more convenient then going to the nearby town centers to watch the movies.

Open air cinemas were common phenomena. I and my siblings fight hard with the other kids to book a favorable place to watch the movies later at night. We lay a mat for the family members to sit later and we take turns to remain there guarding our place until the show begins. We have to take turns to ensure our place was not taken by the others. The shows are shown late at nights. I being young used to sleep off in the midst of the film show.

Sometimes there will be two shows in a row. In that event the first show will begin bout 8.00 pm and the second show will begin at about 11.00 pm. The shows will normally finish around 2.00 am the next morning. During Deepavali days the estate management will grant two days leave for the estate workers to celebrate and be happy. Enjoying and relishing these holidays, the workers are care free and jolly. For us youngsters, it is the best period for joy and gifts.

In addition to the new dresses bought specifically for Deepavali celebrations we also have uncles and aunts giving us small token sums of money as "ang pow money". This "ang pow" money can add up to some big amount. Some of us save it for other days but many prefer to buy sweets and chocolates on the same day itself. The estate retail shop does have a good stream of business during the Deepavali days.

The adults mainly the men folk gather to drink beer or hard liquor at the ready tables provided by the retail shop for these luxury affairs. Some drink excessively and we know for sure they are drunk. The stupor of the drinks makes them talk loudly and for some filmy reasons, a fight erupts amongst themselves. These fights are frightening because they go physical. In their drunken stupor they break the beer bottles to poke their adversary. At times when the quarrels become heated they inadvertently harm their drinking companions' by poking them with the broken bottle. The damages were sometimes fatal and I have witnessed police coming to arrest the worker who had inflicted the injury on the victim.

These workers are always on quarrel modes. A fight will suddenly erupt amongst them for apparent no good reasons. They quarrel for simplest of reasons and I suppose these fights erupt naturally amongst them. Even at times to make a simple decision to choose their favorite popular actors' films for the open-cinema ends into a fight. The popular actors then were Shivaji Ganesan and MGR (M.G. Ramachandran) and the ardent fans of each actor fight over to the choice of these actors. Sometimes the estate management had to intervene to settle their quarrels. To appease both groups a film acted by Shivaji Ganesan and a film acted by MGR are shown respectively. Even for that, fights also erupt to decide which picture was shown earlier.

Sometimes fights also erupt on decision to show Telugu movies or Tamil movies. The Telugus argue that they too were contributing money for the shows and thus they were entitled for Telugu movies but however the Tamils argue that they do not understand Telugu language whilst Tamil is a common language where both the Telugu community and the Tamil community understand watching it.

After the two days of merry making, the estate goes back to normal life. The school children would be hurrying to their respective schools and the workers going to their rubber tapping duties. Life returns to normal and everyone becomes busy with their daily chores.

For the children our daily lives in the rubber estate are a "Deepavali" except that we do not have the pocket money to spend. Most of the people are awake on the mornings around 5.00 am. The mothers were kept busy preparing to send their children to schools and also need to get prepared for work. In the estates both the men folk and the womenfolk work. In the mornings they are awake to begin their respective duties. In households where the children are still toddlers, the elders who are either the men' parents or the wife's parents take care of the toddlers.

At times of temple festivals and marriages, the estate folks gather as a single entity and participate with full enthusiasm and joy. The joy and mirth of the celebration are enjoyed with the idea of togetherness as one big family. During these times visitors from other estates flounder to visit their relatives in the estates. Receiving and welcoming the new visitors are a common joy for all. These visitors are mostly happy feeling welcomed by the estate folk. At times of common bereavements such as funerals or at times of difficulties the comradeship becomes bonded and they are together again.

I shifted to the city when I grew older. I still hear old stories from people like me who have previously lived in the estates. Most of us are nostalgic and have fond memories about the estates we lived in. Many have expressed that life in the estates were mostly trouble free. Need not pay rent for their homes, can have own vegetable gardens, free electricity and free water are provided by the management. Costs of living in the estates were always cheaper than in urban settings.

The father I remember

As I grew into a young man, I used to ask myself the qualities of my father. Was he a good man or a difficult man? Though he was a strict man there were many times I missed him dearly. I loved him dearly for bringing me up strictly. He forced upon me the importance for the pursuit of education. He wanted to see my performance in the form of scoring good marks for the examinations. He praises well when I score good marks and reprimands when I do not.

When young I used to call him as the Rasputin the Mad Monk. Why I nicknamed him as such was due to the fact that Rasputin was fearsome guy in the royal household of the Russian monarch in the 1900's. I heard stories that Rasputin had a charm on the Russian king and he instructed the king to do things as to his whims. Due to that hold on the king, Rasputin used him to kill off many of his known adversaries'. People around the royal household were virtually afraid of Rasputin. They were afraid that they could be the next victim. My father was totally unlike him but due to the fear factor for Rasputin made me associate my father to Rasputin. Both had the fearsome factors in them and that was the reason for associating him with my father. On retrospect my father was never like him at all. It was all my childish imagination which I picked up from a comic book.

My siblings and my friends were also very afraid of him. Some of my friends call him Hitler. So afraid that we shiver when he was in our presence. My friends would run a mile away when they know my father was approaching us. My father was a large man and his fearsome appearance made us fear him.

One day we were playing marbles and that was a great fun for all of us those days. We were busy playing marbles when a boy shouted that "Babu" was coming. Babu was the name given to my father which meant father in the Telugu language. My friends do consider my father as a father too and thus they too call him "Babu". In any instance when a boy shouted "Babu" everyone became apparent that the fearsome Babu is coming towards them. That is enough to run and you must know how they run in fright.

During one of our marble playing session where a good number of about eighteen boys were gathered to play marbles and all were enjoying a good marathon session of an interesting competition between two teams when one buy shouted "Babu coming". That warning cry was enough for the boys to drop their marbles and run helter shelter. In that episode one of the boys tripped and fell upon hearing that my father was coming. He tripped due to the fright. Even now when we reminisce the old stories this episode of "Dinu" the boy who tripped and fell is mentioned until now to describe the fearsomeness of my father.

All my siblings, sister, two brothers and myself were envious of others. Their fathers' were not fearsome as my father. We were so afraid of him that when he was around the house the house would be in pin drop-silence. Sometimes we used to wonder how was that mother could tolerate his fearsomeness. Infect many a times mother has come in for our rescue from my father. My elder brother became a victim many times because my father had branded him as the culprit for any mishaps in the house.

Some of the mistakes I made would have my brother facing the brunt of his canings. Even though my brother protested telling him that the real culprit was me and not him, he would not listen. He rebuked my brother for not accepting the responsibility or not being responsible as an elder brother.

Any mistakes conducted by the younger children are to be borne by the elders. That was the rule my father followed. Many a times I felt sorry for my brother and wanted to admit it was me and not my brother. However the fear I had on my father only made me shiver and I dare not tell. Preferred not to reveal and escape the punishments. My brother being older than me just accepted the beatings to protect us.

As we grew older, we found that he was not so fearsome after all. We chatted on many issues and he gave his views. He always wanted us to succeed in education and was very supportive in getting us any additional books for our revisions. He felt proud in enrolling us into English schools rather than the Tamil schools. He felt proud that his sons were studying in government English schools. Most of our peers were put into Tamil school that was in the rubber estate itself.

My sister being a girl had to study in Tamil school. That privilege was given to boys only. My father's rational was that girls will be married into other families and thus why spend money on them. Otherwise the in-laws would benefit. That was the norm those days. The boys go to English schools and the girls go to Tamil schools. However some parents who do not have the means also send their boys to the Tamil schools.

The formula for boys going to English schools could not be applied wholesale in all households. There are some households where they have more boys than girls will find it expensive. My father could only send me and my elder brother to English schools. My elder sister and my younger brother had to study in a Tamil school. The reason being he could not afford to send all his three boys to government English schools.

The elder siblings stand to benefit in the opportunity for education. The younger siblings get to lose our due to lack of money. Many families could not afford to send all their kids to English schools. Some families do not bother about English education and just send the children to Tamil schools which are in the estate itself. Even to this privilege some parents prefer to have their children help them in the rubber plantation work. These parents never valued education and thus it does not matter whether it is an English school or a Tamil school.

Schooling was a privilege for both the Tamil and English going school children. At least they get to have six years of free education. In the six years they get to learn how to read and write. After six years of formal education then the students need to sit for secondary school entrance examinations. Only those students who get to pass are allowed to enter secondary schools. This hurdle of secondary school entrance examination would sieve out at least 90 % of the students. Most of the students fail and could not achieve the targeted marks to qualify for their entries to secondary schools.

Both my elder sister and elder brother were victims of this difficult examination. They were deprived of secondary school education. My father was strict and angry at my elder brother for failing the secondary school entry examination. He however enrolled my elder brother into a private secondary school to further his education for the next examination at LCE (Lower Certificate Examination). Private education costs money but my father was prepared to spend for my brother's future. Though my father was a strict man he was benevolent when it comes to education.

My sister could not continue to secondary school because she failed in the entrance examinations. Those days it was normal for girls to stop education because they were always needed to do household chores. I was however lucky to continue my education to secondary schools but the secondary school was 23 miles away from my estate.

My younger brother was lucky to continue his education to secondary schools. He was lucky because the entrance examination to secondary schools was abolished when he reached Standard Six. Many students were failing in the entrance examinations and the government wanted to provide a further three years of extra education. This was a better policy because many children who were weak in primary schools made good at the secondary school levels. Some of them even managed to continue their education to higher levels.

My father though was a fierce man and a disciplinarian he had a lot of regards towards education. On his good days he had imparted many a fatherly advice to all of us (his four children). He could find his time during the dinner time when we gathered to sit together.

He told us his exploits from India and how he landed in Malaysia. He migrated to Malaysia (then know as Malaya) with a group of his village friends and relatives. They were tricked to Malaysia by telling them that Malaysia was a land of riches. They could come here and amass wealth in a short period. Only after reaching the shores of Malaysia did he realize that he was short changed of all the promises. His expectations fell short.

To make matter worse as he landed in Malaysia the Second World War began within a short period of him being in Malaya. Malaysia was occupied by the Japanese. During the Japanese occupation, food was scarce and the Japanese currency became worthless. It was during these periods my father narrated to us that he was forcefully sent to the work in the "Death Railway project". The Japanese just came in and rounded up all well bodied youths to work at laying the rail tracks from Burma to Thailand. He told us that many fellow prisoners died there. The British had it worse and every worker was practically bullied to work long hours with little food.

My father narrated to us that when he was doing his work whilst laying the tracks his spade accidently hit the Japanese soldier who was walking by in guard that day. My father immediately bolted into the fringes of the jungle fearing for his dear life. He told us that the Japanese will take such acts though accidental as defiance and they would be quick to cut off one's head.

The Japanese implemented these types of punishment to frighten the public that the same fate could befall them. Hence the public will be obedient to the Japanese. However in my father's instance the Japanese soldier was a kind man and he called my father to return to the camp. My father was relieved and no untoward punishments followed. In other words my father was spared his life. I never knew the Japanese could be that cruel.

One of his strong advices to us was that education is a good avenue for progress. He mentioned that he was slightly better than his father (referring to my grandfather) and he wanted us (the three sons) to be better than him and the only recourse to better him was through education. He did mention that education would pave to us a successful world. We could become doctors, engineers, teachers or any other vocations.

On some other occasions he had advised us to be thrifty and to live within one's means. He advocated a principle that we should never borrow or lend money to individuals. Either way it could spell trouble for us as a lender or as a borrower. As we grew the need to borrow and others wanting to borrow from us became a common situation. In realizing my father's advice I refrained from lending and also borrowing. Until today I advocate and follow his teachings. I am glad that I adhere to it.

Many times my friends complained to me that so and so did not return the money borrowed. There were many times I was quite stuck in this dilemma of the need to lend money or the need to borrow money. Following his wise teachings made me resolute towards either borrowing or lending matters. I just tell my friends that I am following to the tenets of my father's advice and am a stickler to the advice. My friends keep quiet.

One more advice he imparted to me was that hard work pays. He told us never to be lazy and not to avoid work on that account. He advised us "The more work you do the better you become". In reality my present success must be attributed to him for his good advice. Probably my younger days of training have made me strong and even now I do not abhor work. For me work can be a joy. My father himself was a hardworking man. After his demise many people who knew my father described him as a hardworking man. Felt proud of him and he was indeed a hardworking man until his last days. He demised early due to illness.

My father was strict but he showered my sister with a lot of love and affection towards her. She being the only girl for him must have made him soft. He was otherwise to us the boys though he was a bit soft towards my younger brother. Only my younger brother gets the privilege to sit on my father's lap. We were jealous of our younger brother but at the same time we were happy too because we do not get to do so. For me and my elder brother it would be a big relief not sitting on his lap.

My father was stung by a swarm of bees and he was hospitalized due to it. The bee's toxin affected him and he became weak due to the bees' stings. After being discharged from the hospital he started on traditional cures and neglected the western medicines.

I still have a vague memory that my parents believed that some black magic have been casted on him. They suspected his work place enemies must have done the black magic. My parents went hunting for medicine man "bomohs" to remove the spells. My parents spent a lot of money to chase the ghost of false beliefs. On growing up I realized it had been a futile chase and the real truth was that the bee's toxin had not been completely removed and it led to other medical complications.

My father died at a young age of 44 when I was in Form Three. It was very tragic for me and it affected my studies. My results for the Lower Certificate Examination dipped due to the sorrow. I had to endure the emotions of a son losing his father. Due to the lower marks in the LCE (Lower Certificate Examination) I could not enter the science stream even though I was good in my studies.

I was surprised that tears were flowing non-stop on the day of his funeral. I could not understand myself and the sorrow was overwhelming. I fainted many times at the mere thought that he would be no more with us. I was not taken to the graveyard due to my overwhelming emotions on that day. Sons were usually taken to the cemetery grounds to witness the burial.

I later realized that my father's demise was on the 26th June and my birthday was on the 27th June. It made me to make a resolve not to celebrate my birthday ever. For many years I avoided celebrating but sometimes it becomes inevitable amongst the company of friends. My father's demise left an emotional impact on me. I was emotionally convinced that his demise day was purported to tell me to take over the responsibility of the family. My elder brother and I took over the responsibility for the family as the men of the house.

Though my elder brother was the unspoken leader for the family he turned not to be one. My brother slowly drifted to his in –laws side after his marriage and he left the responsibility to me. My father left an indelible impact on me. His teachings of responsibilities' and being accountable to whatsoever I do gave me a deep sense for public duty.

On retrospect my father had laid for me the bridge to achieve success in the field of education. It is in his memory and my reverence for him that I choose to write this book, "The Rubber Tapper's son". He is the rubber tapper and I am the son.

Primary school days

As I mentioned earlier I was of the luckier group who could go to the English schools. Going to English schools were considered as a high standard. Not all children get to attend the English schools. The nearest English school for us was in Batu Kurau, a small shanty town which was about 9 miles away from the rubber estate we were from.

Sending children to English schools was an expensive affair. Parents need to pay fees (about RM 2.50 per student per month) during those days when I was attending the primary education. Nowadays both primary and secondary education is free. Besides paying the fees, parents need to arrange a private car to ferry us to the English schools. Those days we did not have School Bus. Though we had normal buses (called as Time buses), we could not really depend on them. The time buses begin their business operations at 8.00 am which was late. The school begins earlier at 7.45 am in the morning. We had no choice but to engage private cars as our transport to attend the English school. Parents who could afford these expenses would send their children. My father was concerned that we attend the English Schools because he knew then itself that the future lies in English education.

I still remember one Malay uncle (pakcik) who used to ferry us to and fro from the house to school. This uncle sometimes used shortcut which reduces the distance from the rubber estate to the main trunk road. The road that he used was of a hill slope and the road was of a hard terrain and weathered conditions. He was an efficient driver. We used to fear when he comes down the slopes. Adding to that his car was an old car and someone frightened us that old car braking system was bad. However there were times he used to take us on the normal route and we found it was more relaxing. He could send us within 30 minutes for a journey of about 9 miles to the school. The driver of the car resides in a nearby kampong and it seems he usually have some work to do at Batu Kurau and it was just nice for him to finish his work there and then later pick us on the way back. As thus for him it was worthwhile to transport us to school on the weekdays. One good thing of this uncle was his sense of punctuality. He was always early to pick us and he was a kind man. All of us liked him. He had invited us many times to his house to have a feast on his fruits.

My friends who could not afford the English schools always felt envious of us. They used to tease us as "Vellakaren anal karuppu suthu". It literally means that we were Indians but behave like Europeans. It also meant we act white but have black buttocks. However despite all the criticisms and enviousness we remained as friends. We were looked up, but in due time the status goes off when we were at common games.

One particular game I remembered we all loved to play was our own version of football (like footstall) where we used the bottle cap in place of the football. The field is the cement floor of the common open-hall (built for common usage i.e. drama stage shows or talks addressing the estate workers. There will be about four or five in a team. There will be a goal keeper for each team. We kick the bottle cap and pass it to our friends as though it was the football. We will do passing and maneuver the cap towards the designated goal posts. The team that entered most goals was the winner. I wonder whether any youngsters still play this type of "estate football'.

There was another game we fondly played was "Sadu Gudu" which is a form of 'catch the intruder'. In this game the opponent sends their representative to our turf and it is our job to trap him and not to allow him to go back to his territory. We have to pounce on him until he could not utter the word "Sadu Gudu". In the event he can go back all those who were touched or had been in contact with him would have to leave the play as a form of punishment for not being able to apprehend the opponent. In the end the team that had no players left was the loser. That was an exciting game and boys loved the game.

Another game that struck us was playing marbles. In these games we had two types of marble games. One game compromised the colorful marbles and we used to play this game with the notion that when one was able to hit the marble from a specified distance got to acquire the marbles. The sharp shooters mostly won the games and we dreaded to play against the sharp shooters. When we play against them we were bound to lose our marbles to them.

Sometimes we team up where the teams could evenly match with a sharp shooter at each one side. Otherwise we cannot get players to fight against the sharpshooter. When we pair there is a fair chance to win and acquire more marbles. Sometimes we played these game based upon our own teams. We named our teams and the team that played well got to win more marbles. Competitions brew amongst the teams. The teams used to conduct practice sessions to shoot the marbles whereby the sharp shooter could train the juniors as to how to angle and hit the marble. Not to boast I was one of the sharp shooter and I was highly sought by the others to join their teams. Whenever I refused to join my elder brother's team in preference to a friend's team a fight would break out at home. My mother hardly understood as to the cause of the fight. My elder brother however was pretty possessive of me and he was ever ready to come for my defense. He always loved and protected me form the bigger boys.

In the marble category there used to be another set of white marbles. These marbles were more expensive and this game was played by the bigger boys. This game required us to make a hole in the ground and it could be played individually or as a team. The game was to avoid the opposing team from entering their marbles into the hole. When the players turn come up he will try his level best to hit the opponents marble to be further from the hole. Eventually the player who could enter his marble into the hole was the winner.

There were other times we used to dig three holes about three or four feet apart. The contender had to put his white marble in all three holes one after another. The one who managed to complete the cycle earliest was the winner. The loser would have to bear the punishments meted by the winner by having his finger knuckles to be hit by the winner's white marble. It can be painful when the winner was skillful in hitting the knuckles. This game was also engaging.

When the top- season comes along the shopkeeper sells small, medium and large sized tops to the children. Some children choose to make their own tops out of various tree branches. That was the time the guava (jumbo) plants branches were cut off to make the tops. The boys cut of the branches without getting the owner's permission. These guava (jumbo) plants are planted near the vicinity of their houses. They cut the branches at appropriate time when they know they won't be apprehended. The unlucky ones gets reprimanded and scolded.

I and my brother need to make our own tops because our parents will not spare us any money to buy the tops from the shop. Playing tops was exciting and it was filled with fun. The game was to see whose top can last longer. We draw circles and we need to swing and place the top into the circle. Whilst doing so we try our level best to hit the opponents' tops so that it flies out of the circle and disqualify them from the game. The game was also to hit the other's top and spoil it. An expert can split the opponents top into two and emerge as the winner. In this game my elder brother was an expert and he wins most times. In these instances I always prefer to be in his team. Even though he knows I was weak he accepts me into his team willingly. These made me feel guilty because in the marble game I avoided his company mainly he was a liability for me in that game. My elder brother knew about my slyness and till today he reminds me of my misdeeds.

During those good old days we all loved to play-act. We conducted re-enactments of the popular films that were shown in the estates. On days of festivals or monthly good and popular movies on MGR or Shivaji Ganesan used to be shown. They were the popular actors of those days. Immediately the following day we start allocating specific roles to various individuals who are suited for the re-acting. The best part of laughter was when we got to choose the boy to act as the heroine and her friends. We had to choose the boys to play act as girls. We also had a tough time choosing the villain's roles. Everyone wanted the hero's role and none wanted to act as the villain. We even prepared wood swords to make good the fighting scenes we witnessed in the movies. We play- act the movies in the afternoons or at the weekends.

Unfortunately or fortunately we never had any audience to cheer us but it was real fun acting the roles. We learned conversation in Tamil and boasted at our prowess of the language usage. We loved the roles played by Shivaji who was an excellent orator and we loved imitating him. We were far from him. The fighting scenes were mostly monopolized by MGR movies. We play act that too and in the process we were used to getting hurt. Sometimes the fight become real especially when one party inadvertently hit the other and the pain caused him to react in return. When the fight became serious we quickly intervened to stop it. After some time the so called enemies become friends once again.

Girls were not allowed to be near boys neither did they came forward to be near us. They had their own set of games like cooking for a festival or a guest. They preferred to play the "congkak game". They used pebbles or tamarind seeds to play these games. Sometimes the younger girls drew lines on the ground floor and jump accordingly in the boxes on a single leg. These games were popularly called "Nondi" in Tamil. I have seen both the Chinese and the Malay girls playing these games. I wonder what they called it in their respective languages. They have their own version to play the game. They too fight when a fowl was committed. It was interesting to watch girls fight. Their strategy was to pull each other's long hairs. Adults quickly intervene and pull them apart.

Schools were equally interesting because there too we had many friends to play with. This time around we had Malays and Chinese friends to play with. During P.E (Physical education) classes a round ball was enough for us to kick around. Immediately we could form teams to play a good and a hearty game of football on the school field. Hardly had we sweated the bell would ring to inform us the change of period for the next class. All of us look forward for the P.E. classes. The girls play net ball at the net ball court.

Our teachers were good and were good role models. They gave us frequent homework and they were strict to observe that we had completed the homework. Some of my friends who have not done the homework would want to borrow my work in order to copy. Copying was faster because they need not spend time on thinking. They have readymade answers via us.

These lazy friends who frequently borrow my books to copy would treat me with respect and mostly were benevolent to spend for me at the school canteen. I was generally good in my studies since young and my class position never lowered below the 5th position. I and another Malay boy were in stiff competition to clamor for the first position. Though we were good friends but when it comes to marks and examinations we can become bitter competitors. We fight for marks in every subject. I still remember in one instance I beat him to get the first position and his father presented me RM 1.00 (at that time it was considered a big money) as a token of appreciation and also to rebuke his son for allowing me to beat him to the position. I saw my friend (competitor) was hurt and he shed tears. Some other friends frightened me by telling that the father gave me "Charmed Money" so that I won't be able to beat his son in the future. I became frightened because I have already accepted the money. On the same day I told my father about it and he allayed my fear by telling me that my friend's father gave me the money in good faith. He told me that most people respected good students and that I deserved the token money given to me as a reward. Since then I knew the value of education. I was respected both at school and at home, because I was a top scorer in class.

My primary school days were in English and we had a lot of library story books to read. In fact I picked up my reading habit from here henceforth. My richer classmates used to bring in interesting comics' such as Beano, Dandy, Uncle Sam and many others to show off. I got to borrow these wonderful comics and they usually allowed me to take home. I used to read them fast and gave them back on the following day itself. They knew comic books in my hand were in safe hands and in return they can copy the homework given. Studying in the school was a great joy.

After obtaining Grade One in the standard six examinations, my status as a clever student increased. I was getting more attention from parents of school going children. Some of them were well wishers and were proud of me. They encouraged me to study better and make progress in life. Some of them were nice to me because they wanted their primary school children to emulate me and took me as a role-model for their school going children.

Some of them insisted that I guide their children and were willing to pay me tuition fees. At this young age upon their insistence I began to teach their children tuition on reading, writing and arithmetic. I took upon this task because it helped me to have money in my hand and be of a lesser burden to my parents. My father objected of me giving tuition fearing that I would neglect my own studies. However after reassuring my father that I am agreeable with giving tuition and also capable of handling my studies he relented for my wish.

I still remember my standard six class teacher Mr. Ng Kar Tek who was a kind man. He was instrumental for me to score Grade One pass. Those days scoring grade one pass was a big feat. I suppose only two of us (myself and my competitor) got Grade One that year in 1962 for our school. My memory is still vivid when I was called to the stage to collect a trophy for getting the Grade one. I became the talk of the town. I also became the talk of the estate and the nearby estate. I was beaming with joy and pride. My parents and siblings were very proud of me. My father took special care towards me. I realized that hard work pays and the prize I earned was the good marks. Since then I was always been a hard worker when it concerned studies.

All my classmates won't be able to forget Mr. Prasad and his cricket bat. He used to frighten us that if anyone of us misbehaved he would not hesitate to use the cricket bat. Knowing the thickness of the bat we really got frightened because he would use it on us. He himself was a stout figure and his manner of walking was uptight. We all used to shiver at the sight of him. He was the appointed discipline master for the school. When he talks at the assembly it would be a pin drop silence. There were days we knew that he was not around the school and it became a field day for us to make noise. It was just like the parable "when the cat is not around the mouse is the king". However he was a good and a kind man. I knew him so because he was also our prefect master. At the prefect meetings he was very kind and articulate in his instructions. He bought us chocolates and food on good occasions using his own money.

After my Standard Six or rather primary education I had to continue my secondary education at King Edwards VII secondary School in Taiping which was a further 15 miles away from the small town of Batu Kurau where my primary school was located. My primary school was about nine miles away from my rubber estate. My secondary school was 24 miles away from my rubber estate. This was rather far off from my home at the rubber estate but then my father insisted that I should pursue my secondary school education. He always emphasized on education and he wanted to see me as a successful student. It was his ambition and I was determined to fulfill his interest.

I too loved school because it was a place where I got to interact with all my friends. School was mostly fun. Most of the time we were playing and joking. I loved the interval periods because we could rush to the canteen to have our favorite meals. Meals those days were only about 5 cents or 10 cents. Drinks were free because we used to drink the tap water. For 5 cents we can get a round sugar coated ice ball. It is from this ice-ball that the famous ABC (Ais Batu Campur) emerged. Inside the ice ball we had the "red beans (kacang merah)" and like a prized trophy we relished the kacang last. With rose flavored sugar coating and cold sieved iced ball was a favorite for many students. At his hawker- counter for ice-ball at the vicinity of the school canteen it had the longest queue.

I doubt schools sell ice balls anymore but instead they now sell ABC in bowls for reasons of health and cleanliness.

Secondary School days

King Edwards VII Secondary School at Taiping was my next destination to pursue my secondary education. In those days everyone from my district had to go to Taiping to pursue their secondary education.

I still remember there were two boys' and two girls' secondary English schools. There was also a popular Chinese secondary school in Taiping. In total there were five secondary schools which catered for the region of about 30 miles radius. Nowadays secondary schools are everywhere within a radius of about 10 miles and some even lesser.

I still remember that I needed to cycle about 4 miles every day from my rubber estate in the early mornings at about 4.30 am. to a nearby small town which was called as "Batu 20". Here the time bus will reach the place at about 6.00 am from Ijok (another small town which was the last destination point for the bus company). Ijok was about 7 miles away from Batu 20. After boarding the bus at Batu 20, which then plies to Taiping stopping at every place a passenger wants to alight it. It takes about an hour to reach Taiping and stops at my school gate. Hence I normally would reach the school around 7.00 am. The dawn by this time settles down and the atmosphere was being replaced with the sun rise. The sunrise cheered up the environment making it brighter and students begin pouring into the school in the early mornings.

Schools in those days have their schools activities begin at 7.45 am before the time zoning was emplaced in 1982. Nowadays the schools begin their school hours at 7.30 am. There was a shift of 15 minutes earlier from the previous times. The formation of Malaysia gave rise to different time zones being practiced by the people of the peninsula and by the people of Sabah and Sarawak. In order to have a same time zone in all parts of Malaysia the time zone was shifted by 30 minutes earlier for the people of Malaya (then Peninsula Malaysia). As thus all Malaysians experienced the time zone of 8 hours from the Greenwich Meridian. This happened in 1982 during the tenure of Prime Minister Dr. Mahathir Mohammad. He wanted all West Malaysians to begin their day earlier by 30 minutes.

I used to wait outside the school gates in the early mornings. When it rained, we had to take shelter at the bus stops where some kind of shelter was provided. The school gardener would however open the gate much earlier than 7.45 am and would then proceed to open the classrooms. I then would move to my classroom. I used the early hours to read a book or finish doing some homework assignments. My classmates acknowledged that I was one of the earliest to reach school. However there were times when the bus breaks down and the next bus would be an hour later. On those days I would be late to school not for one hour but by about 15 to 20 minutes only.

School finishes around 1.10 pm or sometimes around 1.50 pm. After school we walk to the bus stand at the central part of the town. We then board the bus around 2.00 pm and it reaches Batu 20 around 3.00 pm. At Batu 20, our bicycles would be locked and placed at a trusted shop area. Upon reaching we then take our bicycles and then peddle home for about 30 to 40 minutes. We reached home around 3.30 or 4.00 pm. On Fridays we reach home much earlier. We then quickly take our lunch and then hurry to finish our assignments before night falls. By 9.00 pm we were mostly in the bed fast asleep.

The next day our routine begins day in and day out. Saturdays, Sundays, public holidays and school holidays were joyous for us because we need not wake up so early as 4.00 am in the mornings. We relish the mornings sleep and we warn our parents and siblings never to rouse our morning sleeps. If they do we scold them for waking us up.

There were not many students who were plying to attend schools at Taiping. I remember in my house my elder brother, three other friends and I were doing so every day. My father was particular that we continued schooling and so were our friends' fathers. So one day the fathers discussed as to what should be done. Then they decided to hire a Malay uncle whom we called him as "pak cik". He was willing to ferry us to and fro from home and school every day for a monthly fee. We were happy because we only need to be ready by 5.30 am for the uncle to fetch us unlike earlier where we need to be ready by 4.30 am. We were happy at these arrangements but two of the boys in our group decided to quit school. They cited that they found it was too expensive for them to pay the monthly fees for the transportation. The Pak Cik on the other hand mentioned that it was not economically viable for him to ferry only three students and there is a reduction of revenue for him. As thus he increased his fees and that was to be shared by the remaining three of us. The new arrangement became expensive for my parents. Now the fathers met up again to plan for the next course of action.

This time they planned to make us stay in Taiping itself and we to return to home only at the weekends. They arranged the local goldsmiths shop as our next destination point for us to stay and continue our education. The new place and my school are nearby and we can walk to school. The new arrangements made us lazy because we can now wake up at 6.30 am. and we could be in school by 7.45 am. The goldsmith family not only provided us accommodation (lodging) but also provided us food. I do not how much our fathers' paid them but the new arrangements were rather quite comfortable for us to study in comfort. We could now participate in the afternoon co-curricular activities. Within a span of 15 -20 minutes I was already back to my new home. By 2.00 pm I was already back home unlike my earlier days when we reached home only around 4.00 pm.

Being from a rural primary school I was placed in Form 1 B class and I did not take it well for not being placed into the best class. I was however told by my class teacher that at the end of every year, student's position would be shifted and grouped according to their best performance. I knew this was a good opportunity for me to excel and I worked hard to obtained good results. As thus in the second year itself of my secondary education I got myself to be placed into the Form 2A class. I was very happy and proud that I was now placed in the best of the Form 2 classes.

Form Two classes extended until Form 2D (four classes in total). Though happy I now realized that the students in 2 A here were far much better than me and they were much smarter than me. My position in the class dipped to the twenties unlike in the previous class my position was always above the tens. I had to work harder in order to move up in my position. I worked hard and was never absent from school. I always finished my home work assignments and made sure that I do the necessary reading to be in par with the other smart boys. Eventually I improved my position and gained ground. Competition here at class 2A was challenging. We had to battle neck to neck on the total scores. The competition was really tough but it was a fun and a bitter game. We however knew it was just the examinations and the glory was in surpassing the other. In these games you were the winner sometimes and the loser at other times. These competitions were healthy because it kept me going strong. I was indeed happy when I began scoring good marks on most subjects.

I retained my position to continue studying in the Form Three A class. I made many good friends here and was getting settled with the competitions. Our class teacher was a strict disciplinarian and his meticulousness made me work harder. He was teaching us English. He made sure that we brought in our English dictionary during his classes. Our fear for him was real and we used to shiver in his presence. We nicknamed him as "Hitler" and we were up to date when it comes to his assignments. I still can recite some of the poetry pieces he thought us.

Though he was strict we all liked him because he made sure our class always won the cleanest class competition ever week. The week we lost, we knew we were going to be reprimanded. Students who were on duty for that week and responsible for losing the competition would be reprimanded. They had to present him with extra essays and that was the punishments he gave us. I am however grateful to him because my English usage improved tremendously under his tutelage. He instilled into us the love for poetry and good novels.

We were also blessed with other good teachers when I was studying in this class. We had good teachers all round and they were a good source for motivation. They encouraged us to excel and made us into responsible young adults. I was very happy and my performance was generally good. My grades were improving and that made my parents very proud of me. My friends and siblings were also proud of me. Sometime beginning in March 1966 my concentration in studies declined because my father's health was affected. He was hospitalized for high blood pressure and hypertension. Need to frequent the hospital to take care of him. He was hospitalized now and then. There was a general sorrow at home and my mother was disturbed at my father's declining health. My sister who loved my father dearly was always apprehensive of his health. My brothers too were disturbed and all of us were distressed at the turn of events.

My father had a severe health crisis and in June 26th my father demised. His demise caused uproar at the home front. My whole family went into depression. My sister was a total wreck and she could not take the emotional grief. It was at this juncture my relatives from a nearby estate took the initiative to shift us from the previous estate (my home for a very long period) to another estate. Their rationale was to change the environments for everyone's good. This new home was nearer to my school and since my presence was needed at home I cycled to school.

The new home to school was just about 12 miles away to my school. Taking the time bus was also not an issue because there were more frequent buses from Batu Kurau to Taiping. Over time we could forget our sorrow. We slowly got settled to the new environment. My sister was now normal and she got a job as a rubber tapper in the new estate. My relatives explained to the estate management that I and my younger brother were schooling and thus the need for my sister to work. With the status as a worker and as a contributor for the family, my sister could overcome her grief. She now took over the headship of the house and we reported to her for our financial needs.

My elder brother in order to supplement the family's income became a helping hand at a bookshop in Taiping. He stayed at the bookshop and I used to frequent the shop whenever a need arises to see him. My brother being older would pass me some cash for my expenditure. His pay however was also low and he could not spare much for me. He however would transfer his monthly salary to my mother.

During these periods of turmoil I took a dip into my performance. My school examinations results were poor. I fared badly in the trial examinations. My teacher's noted the decline and requested me to overcome the decline. I made my efforts but did not have much time to catch up with the missing lessons. I have lost out in understanding the concepts needed in science and mathematics'. Tried to do more on these subjects but as I mentioned earlier, the time was insufficient to catch up with the studies. Though I passed my Lower Certificate of Education (LCE) with a Grade One the overall results declined. Due to this decline I could not enter the science stream. The seats in the science stream were normally given to students who performed well in the public examination. Though sad I accepted to the sad reality that performance was the yardstick for placements.

I was placed into Form Four A 3 being the next best class after the science stream. There was only one class for the science stream and there were three other classes for the arts stream. In class Form Four Arts 3, Principles of Accounts and Commerce were thought in this class. Other two Form Four Arts 1 and Form Four Arts 2 classes did not have these subjects to offer. These classes were offered different subjects. It was here that my life's foundation was beginning to be set. I was showing a liking for Principle of Accounts and Commerce. It interested me to know the business world. It was the beginning of my horizon towards the business aspects that was being conducted by so many business firms in the country. It was here that I learned about company shares and debentures. Again shares itself have different format of shares. My Accounts teacher thought us how to look at the business section and see the Index on the share price fluctuations from the daily 'New Straits Times'.

There was an offer by the school for students intending to pursue science subjects and who have scored good marks in mathematics and science subjects are welcomed to join the science class. I was one of the lucky boys who were offered a place in the science class. Most of my friends from Form 3 A were in the science class. I knew competition would be tough in the science class. However the Principles of Accounts and

Commerce interested me and moving to the science class would deprive me from pursuing the Accounting line of education. As thus I remained in Form Four Arts Three. It is a new world for me. By them the sorrows due to the demise of my father was forgotten and I was committed towards doing well in my studies.

At this juncture of my life, my school principle, Mr. Long Heng Hua took me and two other friends under his care. All three of were from poor families and our homes were reasonably far from school. Another common feature all of us had in common was that we were good in our studies. Due to these reasons we were offered a place in the School hostel.

This hostel was only meant for the Malay students whose homes were also far away from school. The monthly fee for the hostel was only RM 15.00 per month which included both lodging and food. To be frank it was a luxury for all three of us to be offered a place at the school hostel. We learned to live with the Malays and had no racial issues with them. The hostel offer was one of the best things I have obtained in life. My lifelong gratitude goes to Mr. Long Heng Hua. Life at the hostel provided me with a lot of benefits and I made many friends here. It provided me an impetus to improve my education to a higher level.

I joined the debating society and many other co-curricular activities. I could not join the football team because there were always better players than me. Likewise I got myself rejected from the hockey team. However I got myself selected to join the school cricket team. I was lucky to be selected because not many students were interested in cricket and I had friends in the team. I joined the school scouts and learned a few things here.

My school, King Edwards VII Secondary school was a popular school and due to that we had regular competitions with other schools. I could only represent the school in cricket. However when it came to annual school sports I could at least represent my "Parr House" in some athletics events and some games. Life in the school was really occupying. Back home at hostel, we needed to finish our homework assignments and do our own studying. Though we had leisure time it went towards playing football at the school hostel football field.

Time really flew fast and the time to sit for the "Senior Cambridge" examination began in 1968. As expected I got Grade One with a few subjects' scoring distinctions. I did very well in all the subjects excepting Principles of Accounts where I failed. I got an F 9 (Failed) for this subject. For Commerce I got a distinction pass. In that year I was the only student who failed in Principle of Accounts, otherwise we would have got a 100 % pass in this subject.

I was remorseful and went forward to apologize to my Accounts Teacher, Mr. Kong. He was surprised too and in his estimate he could not believe because in the Trial Examination I have got a distinction. He wanted to recheck the paper with the Examination syndicate. Those days our papers were marked in Cambridge (England, United Kingdom) and due to the long process we decided to abandon the complaint. I was eligible to move up to pursue Form Six, due to my good results. Only qualified students were allowed to move up to pursue Form Six classes. Since I had this legibility to go Form six, I decided not to proceed to recheck my paper. Most probably I must have answered wrongly because I could not balance the accounts. Some flaw must have had happened.

Going to Form six was an interesting experience. Now I belonged to the school elite. We were looked up by the other students. For the Indian students I became an 'Annan (big brother)" and that was how they used to refer to me. Another interesting feature of Form six classes was that we had girls in the class. My class was now filled with both girls and boys. In the beginning I was very shy of them but in due time we all became good friends.

Form six classes were a new experience and we studied differently. The teachers got us prepared to discuss and then present the discussions It was interesting because it encouraged self learning. The Form six students need to spend more time in the library making notes. We used to clamor for the good books and we had to do a lot of reference work.

I developed a great liking for World History and Economics. The General Paper was also an interesting subject because it entailed a lot of healthy debates amongst us. The teachers were encouraging us to do self study and they told us that the days of spoon feeding were over.

As I was enjoying the feel of the Form Six classes, the environment at home front was hit by economical hardships. My family could not support my studies and sister had to get married. Though sister was willing to sacrifice her marriage to ensure I finished my studies first did not go well into my immature mind.

I did not have any elders who could guide us into the new dilemma. I felt that my sister should not sacrifice her marriage prospects due to my continuing studying in school. I did not want to burden my family and thus decided to end my studies abruptly. At that particular time of my leaving the school my principal Mr. Long Heng Hua was oversees attending some important meeting. If he knew I was stopping my education he would have definitely stopped me from leaving the school at such a critical period. However I left school when I was half way through the Lower Six.

I still remember vividly when I was in the Lower Six Form in the year 1969; there were a lot of public furor on the Landing of Man on the moon on July 21st 1969. It was a great phenomena and a human feat for the landing of Neil Armstrong on the moon. Everyone was talking about it. During this period I was residing at the school hostel.

On that particular day of the moon landing we were having a lot of school activities. My school had also visited another school for a football match. On that particular night of the moon-landing sometime around 12.30 pm when most of the hostel boys have had gone to bed I went over to the hostel balcony to look at the moon. I wanted to have a look at the moon to witness the first landing of man on to the moon from the balcony. It was a bright moon and wondered upon the greatness of man to having made the attempt to land on the moon. After looking at the moon I went back to my bed and it was the hostel rules not to put on the lights after 10.30 pm.

The hostel rules wanted all students to be on bed by then. Due to this factor I did not put on the lights and since there was moonlight, the darkness was manageable for me to walk to the balcony without much help.

After watching the moon I walked back to my bed but due to my mind being preoccupied with the moon landing I mistakenly went to my neighbors' bed instead. I was inadvertently looking for the pillow to rest my head. My big dark hand was searching for it but instead it landed on my neighbor's face. My neighbor let out a loud wail screaming "Hantu" (Ghost in the local Malay language) and in his fright kicked me. His feet landed on my chest and since it was a hard thud I went sprawling to the floor. Instantly someone put on the lights. There was a big confusions as to what has happened and in the midst of this commotion I remember one of the footballers who also shared the same dorm came over to our bed but due to his fatigue and in his drowsiness he lied down on the floor and slept there and then.

It was quickly diagnosed by all that an evil spirit (Ghost) has caused this disturbance. The following day the hostel steward made inquiries and resolved the issue by declaring that the culprit was me and all to relax and that there was only a mishap and no ghost had visited us. It was a big joke and became a day's talk all over the school.

However the story of the "Hantu" visiting us at the hostel frightened the Form One dorm boys. They pulled their beds closer and in fear they were sleeping closer to avert the fear of the "Hantu". It was an interesting happening in the school and then stories started that the bathroom was haunted and that the boys have witnessed dogs howling and running around chasing an unknown figure. I suppose these stories are still circulating in the school hostel. For me it was an interesting episode and until today I am still narrating the story to my family members and friends as to this funny episode of my life.

On retrospect's I really enjoyed the days at the school hostel and at the school. Life at school provided me a good avenue for character building. Studying in a renowned school at King Edward VII Secondary School was my good privilege. It was one of the top echelon secondary schools in the country both in stature and in tenure.

Life in a rubber estate

The population in my estate could be about 200 plus workers and with their children the estate could be harboring about 500 people in total. I still admire the rubber trees. I suppose it is a legacy left by the British colonizers in Malaysia. The fondness for the rubber trees began very early in my life. During Saturdays, Sundays or during school holidays' I go down to the rubber fields to help my mother or father. I help them in their task to tap about 250 – 300 trees per day. When I was in my primary school days I was not allowed to tap the rubber trees. It seemed that that I lacked the skills to tap the rubber trees and could possibly injure the bark of the trees. My job then was to clean the latex bowls which retained the deposits of previous days' latex. That saves time and the tapper can go to another tree at a faster rate and he can get to finish the tapping by 10.30 or 11.00 am. For some good reasons, taping the rubber trees is done mostly in the mornings only.

As I grew to become a teenager I was allowed to tap the rubber trees because by then I have already acquired the skills to tap the soft bark accordingly. Even that we only tap when the supervisor (Kangani) or the conductor was not around. The management does not allow others to tap the trees. I was a better rubber tapper than my parents'. I could tap more trees than them within the similar period of time. I liked tapping and enjoyed to watch the flow of the latex to the cups. Later part of the day we had to collect the latex. I enjoyed noticing some of the trees yielding a lot of latex to the brim of the latex clay cup. Some trees need to be equipped with two cups.

Besides helping my parents in the fields I too had a great admiration to the rubber trees. The rubber trees are planted in neat rows and at equal distance. In a flat land the rubber trees display a neat row of trees and it was a sight to watch. It reminded me of my school cadet corps lined up getting ready for the rehearsal march. The rubber trees of similar trunk size and its picturesque display make the rubber trees a sight to watch. Many of my friends have commented about this array of rubber trees.

Life in the rubber estate brings me many fond memories and sometimes when I hear old songs rendered over the radio makes me nostalgic of the life in rubber estate. The relationship with the old Tamil songs and the rubber estate was because when the songs emerged into the music world my residence was in the rubber estate then. Some of the popular songs were also witnessed via the open air cinema screens.

The then popular actors were MGR, Sivaji Ganesan, Gemini Ganesan, Jai Shankar and many others. The popular villains were Veerapan, Nambiar and Asohan. Their films most often carried melodious songs as a part of the script. Even now when the old songs were aired it brings me old memories. Watching these movies were a luxury for the rubber tappers and their children. They used to show at least one good movie a month via the open air cinema concept.

During periods of festivals we used to get two movies one after another. It brought us great joy. We wait eagerly for the movies but most of us when we get to watch the second movies would have slept off. Sleeping at 1.00 am was never our norm and being children we most often slept off. Even adults avoid seeing both the movies. However movie freaks will make sure that they see both the movies because to them watching movies was the best entertainment they get. As for me I grew up watching these movies that has had a lasting impact in my life. My love for music and good songs all grew from here. I also like the story lines of the movies. Until today I am an avid movie goer because of this experience.

There was a Tamil school in my estate where my sister and my younger brother studied. All those who could not afford to study in the English schools were sent to study in the Tamil schools. There were only two teachers catering for all the students. I am still wondering how the two teachers divided their job scopes. They had to cope with the all the students from standards one till standard six. I came to know that Standard one, two and three were combined. The higher standards Four, five and six were combined.

The teacher's weapon was the cane and they probably could have used them wisely because they could manage the classes with good discipline. Most students were afraid of the teachers. My sister used to tell me who and who got caned that particular day. Due to that the students were in virtual fear of them. Some students excelled because they really feared the teacher's wrath. I was fortunate that I need not adhere to such strict disciplinary actions. I was fortunate that primary days in Batu Kurau went smoothly. Batu Kurau is a small town where the English School was situated and it was about 9 miles (12 kilometers) away from the rubber estate where I lived.

In the afternoons when we were free from school work we boys would gather to play our own games. We have choices to play kites, marbles, tops and many other games. We even re-acted out the films that were previously shown in the open air cinema. We nicknamed each other and made fun of them. The provoked guy would fight back and a new fight will ensue. Soon supporters gather for each fighter and it erupts to become a gang fight. Sometimes the elders intervene and break up the fights.

As we grew older our games changed. Instead of playing games we used to go fishing. Our fishing method involved physical work, where we blocked the stream flow. We practically drained out the water by building dams and pouring out the water from the area where we targeted fish should abound. In that way the fish are trapped and have no escape route. We then pick the fish we want, leaving the small fish back. After that we open back the dam to make the water flow normal again. In this manner we could pick about thirty to forty fish. We then share the fish according to the number of people involved.

In the afternoons' we gathered to play competitive football. Most of us were bare-footed because we could not afford football boots. We played hard because we want our teams to win. We could get a good coach from the Tamil school teachers or the estate conductors. Otherwise we ourselves played according to our own knowledge.

Life in the estate had many advantages. When there was a wedding in one of the households, the youths in the estate would gather to do a lot of errands. Amongst them would be to make a tent of coconut leafs. The cover of the tent is normally supplied by the estate management office. The decorations using coconut leaves and mango leaves would need the skills of the youngsters to do the makeup. We also find pair of banana trees to tie at the entrance of the tent adjoining to the house proper. It was immaterial whether it was the bride's house or the bridegroom's house. Sometimes lovers from the same estate get married and we then would need to do the decorations at both the houses. In addition to the green leaves we also focused to beautify the house by putting decorative colored papers at the tent area, main hall and the bedroom.

It was fun doing the decorative work. We got to spend the evening hours at the wedding house in full merriment disturbing either the bride or the bridegroom. We also get to play cards when there is a quorum of more than four people to open a table to play cards. Mostly the card games are done after the decorations are done. There will be a free flow of coffee or tea from the wedding house. Some tidbits, biscuits or cakes will also be provided as our incentives to do the decorations. Some of the senior youths join us at the later part of the evening mainly to play cards. Small bets are placed as the gambling begins.

Likewise when a tragedy strikes a household in the form of an accident or death the youths again gather to do whatsoever work that was required of them. It is immaterial whether the household is their enemy or not they are cooperative in quickly organizing what so ever the household would need to reduce their burden on the event that hit them. They would quickly put up the tents and will do the necessary arrangement that befits the occasion. Even coffin boxes are made by them. They also stay vigil for the night by taking turns. To stay awake they play cards with small bets to keep the game exciting. The following day when the funeral rites begin there will be providing the farewell dance for the departed. Fire crackers are sometimes lit and drums are played to announce to the neighborhoods that the funeral precession was about to begin.

Those were the days of the estate life where mirth and joy are part of our lives in the rubber estate. Compared to urban living these gathering of people at short notice is a difficult task. The comradeships in the estates were always close. The same story prevails in most rubber estates. I have friends whose youth days too had been in the estates and we are all agreed that comradeship in the estates were close and good. The sense of brotherhood was good and all of us do realize that this part of cooperation was missing in the urban settings.

Most estates during my time were members of the Plantation Union and occasionally the union leaders would attend the estates to give some talks on the worker's rights and the need for solidarity to be members of the Plantation union. I still remember in one instance that there was a worker's protest for some pay demands. During that period there were frequent visits of the Union officials visiting the estates. There was a huge fanfare of a big congregation of workers in the estate. Even the workers from the neighboring estates were present to hear the talk of this official from the Plantations Union. If I was not mistaken it was PP. Narayanan who was the official who came to give the big talk. I did not understand what he was talking but there were frequent claps indicting a big support for his movement.

I asked my father was this official (PP. Narayanan) more important than the estate white manager. My father then replied that this official was a national leader and he had much greater powers than the estate manager. Then only it knocked some sense into me that Indians too can be greater than the white managers. He explained to me that the Union was fighting for equal wages for both men and women. At that time the women were paid less than the men. I remembered then that the following day all the rubber tappers were on strike. It was a national phenomena and I heard from my friends that most rubber estate workers abstained from work for one long week. It affected the productivity of rubber production.

To mitigate some expenses for feeding the families the union organized mass cooking whereby all families could come to eat there. During these periods of strike the workers families were feeding on the mass cooked food. My father told me it was meant to keep the workers in solidarity and motivated for the ongoing strike. In the end the strike was successful and the strike was called off. The Plantation industry leaders agreed to pay the women equal wages. The news was printed in all major newspapers and it was a success for the efforts of the Union officials. Upon hearing the positive news the whole estate was in a joyful mood. This indicates that the household income would now increase because both men and women get same wages. As thus there was an increase of wages for the household. No wonder there was a great rejoice amongst all the workers.

Estate life had many shared memories. Though the workers need to wake up and be at the work site as early as 6.30 am they get to come back from work as early as 12.30 pm. It was considered as a day's work done. The rest of the time until the next day was their time. Some men are enterprising because they reared goats and cattle. As thus they can be occupied in cutting grass or doing other related jobs for cattle or goat rearing. Some men do market gardening to cater for the vegetable demand amongst the estate folks.

My father had a vegetable farm and my father's favorite crop was the egg plant. We could sell the produce to the estate households. Another popular crop we used to plant was lady's finger and long beans. I used to admire my father who single handedly has planted many plants that were more than to my family requirements. My mother was the saleswoman and she gets orders from other womenfolk. I was the bill collector. My mother gives me a list of people, who owed us from the purchases they made. The moment the payday was up I would be required to collect the arrears from the customers. Most of the times I could collect the moneys owing. However there were times I could not collect the money. My mother would then venture to collect the amount owing. Most of the times, she would be successful in the collections.

Some men indulge into drinking habits and they drink hard liquor from various brands. These are the men who frequently ignored their families. Most of their money was spent on the drinks. Some of these men were addicted to drinks and they are the ones who requested the wives to give them the money. When the wife refused to give the money a fight ensued. Some of these men were rough in handling these matters and they resorted to violence to extract the money.

These families endured their hardship by depending on the wife's income. These are the children who emulated their father's footsteps and picked up drinking at the tender age of 15 years. There are many cases similar to these. I have personally witnessed many such families who endured their father's addiction to drinks. In most instances these are the families that become trouble makers for the Indian community. The children from these families were the biggest contributors for the mischief.

During the pay days which were normally on the 7th and the 20th of the month there would be a lot of activities. One of them would be the creditors going after the workers who owed them money. It was interesting to watch as to how the workers dodge their creditors in trying to avoid paying. It was also the occasion where the men could afford boozing with the extra cash in hand. In this instance the worker spends a bulk of their salary on the drinks that day itself. The wives would be very angry and they would be fighting with their husbands for the extravagance in spending the bulk of the money with little considerations for the household expenses. Fights also ensued due to drunkenness and stupor of the liquor. In all these instances I used to be proud at my father for not subjecting himself to the above follies.

My respect for him for him was well placed. He always gave his priority to his family's needs. He was a responsible man and respectable amongst our community. When the other men are busy gulping the beer with their friends my father will only buy one small bottle of beer for his consumption on the pay days. Sometimes he buys toddy but he never exceeded his limit above one pint of toddy. For that I should salute my old man and due to that I never missed paying respects to my father's anniversary every year. I visit the temple on the particular day and make an earnest prayer thanking him for his guidance and molding me as a good citizen.

The essence of the rubber estate life was the bond ship we have amongst all the families. Though there were quarrels amongst us but we always patched up during times of hardships or tragedies. The workers always lent a supportive arm to the grieving party. During these trying times the estates folks do live as a community to forgive and forget. These phenomena was absent in urban living.

Scandals and rumors were many in the estate life. As a student I was used to hearing of scandals of husbands and wives having affairs with other men and women. Though all behaved as perfect angels their individual stories come flying during periods of quarrels. However these scandals were not related to all people in the estate. Only the people who seem to be more promiscuous would need to carry the burden of the smear campaigns. Sometimes these rumors also flourished due to enmity or jealousy and the victims were purposely targeted. I suppose this type of issues are time memorial and happens in all generations. These rumors added spice to our life in the rubber estates.

Running to Kuala Lumpur (a City of hope)

I am a victim of sheer stupidity. I left school for no good apparent reason. When I reminiscent as to why I had left school in a hurry when most things were going in my favour made me aware of the stupidly I mentioned earlier.

It was not poverty that made me do the haste decision. I was not being honest to cite poverty as the reason for me leaving my form six classes because my family could afford the school fees. On retrospect I should have no piety or excuse for leaving school abruptly but it had happened. Only reason that I could express was that I was beguiled by the newspapers and their false reporting. I trusted the newspapers then. I still have doubts on their truth in their reporting or was the reporting based upon the opinions of the reporters.

When I was in Form six in the year 1969, the papers carried stories mentioning that the country was going through a recession and that jobs were difficult to come by. The recession was so bad until even university graduates were finding it difficult to get jobs. That reporting frightened me as a student.

In my immature and young mind, I got worried and afraid that I too would not be able to get a job even though I could become a university graduate. Why study when cannot get a job. That was my logical thinking and these rational made me to leave school. I lied to the school authorities that my family was finding it difficult to pay my fees and support my education. They believed my sob story. It was rather unfortunate for me that during this time of me applying to leave school, my principal (headmaster) was in England attending some conference. Otherwise he would have interfered and would have stopped me from leaving the school. Reasons of poverty would not have convinced him. He would have found some other alternative financial aid for me to depend on.

Some of my Form Six teachers and classmates were quite concerned for me leaving school in the midst of the year. I applied to leave sometime in August 1969. They threw caution to me telling me that it was not easy getting a place to study Form Six and it was stupid abandoning it half way. They assured me that it would be better to endure one more year and leave after Upper six. They advised me that the Higher School Certificate would be useful for job applications or other opportunities. My fellow hostel mate who is now a medical Professor Dr. Maniam was my good friend. He too advised me strongly not to leave school. It was real silly of me to have rushed into making the decision to leave school. My family too was stunned and surprised that I had applied to leave school.

I was enjoying my school life as a form six student. It was during this period I became a vivid reader of the daily newspaper. It was the main newspaper that had caused me such turmoil. I was staying in the school hostel and we got regular supply of newspapers being subscribed by the hostel. It was this paper reading that influenced me to leave school due to the negative reporting.

It reported that graduates could not find jobs and that the country's economy was dipping. Times were bad and that everyone was suffering. It was here the devil was stirring my innocent mind to leave school. Frankly I believed those fears and that caused for my decision to leave school. However responsibilities towards family were also a cause. I could not stand watching my mother working to support my education. My sister who was working as a rubber tapper then was also contributing towards the family and she was my main benefactor to sponsor my education. Marriage proposals were refused by her due to the reasons of me studying. She knew that her presence was necessary to support my education.

During those days it was not a norm for Indian girls to marry late. I became worried that her reasons of rejecting marriage proposals would one day make her an unmarried spinster and that was due to me being a student. I did not want to burden her and become the cause for her non-marriage. When my brother-in- law came to propose for my sister's hand and before my sister could even reject him for the marriage proposal I resigned from school. This gave my sister no choice but to marry. My brother in law was a good caring man and he took good care of my sister and their marriage was a good one. The thought that she could have become an unmarried spinster if only I had not left school half way frightened me. I was silly and stupid but when I watched my sister's happy marriage made me feel happy. It was worth the sacrifice.

After getting my school leaving certificate, I made preparations to come down to Kuala Lumpur and was a guest to one of my family friend. This family friend assured me that he could get me a job in Kuala Lumpur being the capital of Malaysia. I arrived in Kuala Lumpur and managed to locate my benefactor. He was at home to receive me. We exchanged notes on the common people we know.

To my surprise my host was leaving Malaysia for good on the following day. It seems he had to move out due to mounting debts he owed people around. He however introduced me to another family friend of his to provide me the accommodation at their place after his departure. The new family was good and took good care of me. However I had no job or school to go. I remained idle for a few days and as a temporary gap measure I got a job to work as an usher in a cinema theatre. The job was interesting but the pay was low. Got to watch free movies.

My fellow workers at the cinema theatre which was my work place were jovial characters and we had a good time working together. During times of non interesting shows the cinema hall used to be empty having only a few patrons. However there were times when some interesting movies were shown when the tickets used to get sold out. I learned about black marketing. Some speculators buy tickets in advance and then resell them at a higher price for people who could not buy tickers from the theatre's management. These racketeers made some fast buck here.

We the workers were not allowed to sell any tickets in the black market. However we were smart in our own way. We put in spare chairs in the theatre for people to pay and watch. The cinema patrons do not mind these arrangements. They did not want to miss the shows because they have already made their efforts to watch. Furthermore they prefer being a pioneer to watch the movie early which will add their status as early birds. We as the workers share the money collected from the cinema goers via these special arrangements. They paid us the money for making the special arrangements for them to watch the movies. During times of screening good movies our illegal revenue could be good and sometimes it exceeded our wages.

My life as a cinema usherer only lasted for three weeks because I got a job as a temporary teacher in Kuala Terengganu. I packed my bags and was on the way to Kuala Terengganu for new hope and new joy. I was asked to teach Principles of Accounts in a private school. It was more like a tuition centre then a school because it was being housed in a shop house. I was given free accommodation at the back of the shop house or rather the school. It was my job to open the school premise for the days' learning and teaching.

Quite immediately I had a class of 15 students who were keen to learn Principle of Accounts. I must have been a good teacher because more students were joining the class. The enrollment reached to forty students and the owner decided to break the class to two classes. I was beginning to enjoy the job as a teacher but a new impediment came in to my detriment. The owner of the private school wanted me to sign an agreement for two years. I was in a dilemma because two years could be long and life in Kuala Terengganu could be lonely. I was already feeling lonely with very few friends there. My life in Kuala Terengganu was short lived. The owner did not want to have me unless I signed the contract. I only lasted here for one month and was back again to Kuala Lumpur, the City of Hope.

Upon my return I applied for a job at Sime Darby Malaysia Bhd. As an accounts clerk. I was selected and was chosen to assist an accountant from Singapore. At that time we had to depend upon Singapore for company management work. Sime Darby Malaysia was adopting Data Analysis or rather computerization of its accounting records. It was moving away from manual accounting towards computerization of its accounting. A team of accountants from Singapore were down in Kuala Lumpur to introduce the new system of accounting. I was placed directly under one of the Singapore accountant. He was a good boss. I learned fast and infect was faster than the other staff who were having difficulties moving away from the old manual system to the new computerized accounting. For me everything was new and did not have any issues in learning the new system.

Being young I could pick up the various computer codes that were being used to represent the various accounts. I can still remember the Code 8327 was used for Salary Suspense Account. My boss was apparently was using this salary suspense account heavily to rectify a lot of discrepancies in the system of transferring the records of manual accounting towards computerized accounting. Over a short period I could remember the codes for most of the accounts. I was quite like a walking dictionary because most of the codes were known to me. I was mostly sought by my fellow workers for these codes.

Being proactive and in eagerness to earn more money via overtime I quickly had my position moved up from being temporary Accounts clerk to become permanent Accounts clerk.

My Singapore boss quite liked me and could realize he was relying on me most of the times. He suggested that I take up Professional Accountancy and due to his constant harassment for me to pursue further education I applied to sign in as a student to sit for the ACCA (Associate Certified Chartered Accountant) examinations. Being young and energetic I was becoming popular in my Accounts Department. Life was good here.

In those days a teacher's job was looked high and many people respected teachers. I had quietly applied for Teacher's training college and went for the interview. I was selected to become a teacher and soon I got marching orders to report to the Specialist Teachers Training Institute at Cheras, Kuala Lumpur as a trainee teacher.

Meanwhile I had worked in Sime Darby Malaysia Bhd. for a period of one year and made arrangements to apply for resignation from my job as an Accounts clerk. My Singapore boss was startled when I told him that I was going to leave my job. He quickly dissuaded me and reminded me that I have already enrolled for the professional examination and the future here was better.

I agreed to leave a good job in a secured multi-national big firm because to become a teacher in a government school had been an ambition for a long time. My mother too preferred me as a teacher. Since there is an offer, I felt it was only proper and wise to accept the teacher's job. I left the Accounts clerk job with a heavy heart because "Teacher's" job carried status and furthermore I was moving up to realize my dream job. I was happy to become a teacher.

Moving around without directions

Having an elder who is wise in the family is essential. I did not have anyone upon whom I could have depended for guidance. In my case I did not have family elders who were educated. Much anguishes and sufferings could have been easily avoided if only I had someone to depend upon and seek advice.

Leaving school abruptly made me realize as to the importance of consultations I should have sought upon anyone elderly for guidance. It is important to seek guidance from elders or senior friends because as a young person we are bound to make mistakes. These mistakes take time to rectify them. To quote as an example. If I had followed the norm of finishing my Form six studies and proceeded to finish undergraduate studies, I would have finished doing so by the year 1973. However due to the ignorance of not seeking proper guidance I had to work hard to rectify my ignorance and become a first degree graduate in the year 1983. I have burnt ten long years on an unnecessary long journey.

After finishing my teachers training college, I applied to attempt for my Higher School Certificate and it took me three years to complete. I got my STPM (Sijil Tinggi Pendidikan Malaysia) in 1976. I then went to pursue for a degree education at the public universities. Unfortunately I was not accepted into these universities because I did not have a credit in Bahasa Malaysia.

The rules have changed and there was a request that only students who possessed a credit in Bahasa Malaysia were eligible to be admitted into the public universities. I did not have a credit in Bahasa Malaysia because in our SPM days in 1968 there was no Bahasa Malaysia but only Bahasa Kebangsaan. The Ministry of Education then upgraded the status of Bahasa Malaysia from Bahasa Kebangsaan. It was mandatory that I had to take the Bahasa Malaysia paper to get my credit pass and then apply for the public university intake.

Meanwhile ICSA (Institute of chartered secretaries and Administrators) came into my life as a savior. This Institute does not require any credit in Bahasa Malaysia. Furthermore ICSA has been recognized by the government as a Degree and the government could upgrade my statues as a graduate teacher. I ventured to take ICSA as my future path.

I studied at home with little guidance from any academic institutions because there were none catering for part-timers during those days. I had to study on my own. Students who went and studied at formal institutions could achieve success after three years. In my case because it was a self study attempt, it took me five and half year to complete the program. I passed the examinations and was issued the status as Graduate Chartered Secretary and Administrator. I was fortunate the government recognized it as a graduate degree in the teacher's salary scheme.

Since my ICSA (Institute of Chartered Secretaries and Administrators) qualifications were recognized as a MQA (Malaysian Quality Assurance) approved degree I was absorbed into the Teaching scheme as a graduate teacher. I was happy to achieve the new status as a graduate teacher in the year 1983. If I had not left school in 1969 and had listened to the advice of any knowledgeable elders I would have graduated in 1973. Since I had no elders to advice I only graduated in 1983 instead of graduating in 1973.

I was ten years behind and that affected my stages in life. I did not want to marry until I graduated and that was the reason for me to marry late. I married at the age of 32 and it was considered late as per the general Malaysian standards then. However I am grateful to the universe for allowing me to have a pair of good children. My daughter is a doctor now and my son is an architect. In my view everything that happened, happened for the best. The general theme that "it is better late than never" was apt for me.

A family that has a wise elder in its midst is an asset for them. The elders could guide the youngster as to the right path they could take in their journey of life. Consultations with them could thwart them of any misfortunes that could arise due to ignorance encountered by the youths. The elders who apparently were more street wise could give the right directions to the youngster. I was unfortunate that I did not have one to depend upon. If not the mistake of leaving Forms six haphazardly would not have taken place at all. The family elder would be there to guide and give wise directions to their young.

There were many moments I was pinning for the presence of my father. He could be there to offer me proper advice. I remember in my primary school days my father was always there for me to depend upon. His demise during my formative years of growing up was a big loss for me. I grew up in the company of women who are my mother and sister. My sister and mother were there to provide me money and support during these periods. Their feminine influence on me had an effect on me. I always felt that I could not make decisive decisions like a man firmly. My decisions were always flimsy and undecided just like most women.

I would consider this as a weak characteristic of my personality. It affected my leadership skills and was never in the front line to be an autocratic leader. I always remained as a second line- leader. Whenever I was appointed as a leader in any organizations, I would quickly decline the offer. However when I was appointed for the post to be the secretary or treasurer I have accepted these posts because I would not be in the front line administration. Only much later did I realize that this weakness had been detrimental for me. With the passing of time I have now recovered from this inferiority feeling.

My teacher training college days

My days at the Teacher's training college were the best part of my formative life. I had applied to the Ministry of Education for teachers training. I was fortunate to be selected and was sent to the Specialist Teachers Training Institute at Cheras, Kuala Lumpur. The two years as a teacher trainee in college went by as a daily bliss. From morning until dusk or rather to bed was filled with laughter and jokes.

Our lessons were conducted in English and the lecturers were of high standard. I realized that they were particular in imparting good knowledge to us and it was apparently useful for my days as a teacher in secondary school. We were introduced to child and adolescent psychology that were a relevant knowledge for us to use when we were dealing with the school teenagers.

My group was particularly chosen to teach Physical Education (Pendidikan Jasmani) and Commerce (Perdagangan) in secondary schools. Due to the nature of our intended training we were required to spend the mornings in the fields to learn the rudiments of the games and athletics. We were taught the rules of every sports game and the rules pertaining to athletics. Even swimming was included into the syllabus. Mock games were being played by us to understand the games better. The girls had different games to follow and we normally got ourselves divided when it involved the games. At times the class was combined when the knowledge was necessary to be imparted to both the groups.

In the latter part of the mornings we had classes on child psychology, theories on education and other relevant matters. Lessons in Bahasa and English was also maintained and imparted to us. In the afternoons we had classes on Principles of Accounting, Commerce, Economics, shorthand, Trengkas (Malay shorthand) and typewriting. Our days were packed with classes and we only had breaks for tea and lunch. The classes stop at 5.00 pm and we were required to participate as referees for other course mates when they had games in the evenings. The idea was to practice what we learned in the mornings.

Our classes were packed with quality dissemination of information and assignments. Our lives in the college were filled with fun and joy. Though we had assignments to do we still had time for fun and frolicking. In the late evenings we gathered at the "Congo Bar".

We nicknamed a Malay restaurant as "Congo Bar" and we enjoyed their food itineraries such as "mee rebus", "roti canai" and "teh tarik". The Congo Bar was our landmark place at the outskirts of our college. We used to adjourn here for late supper with our group members. It was here we can witness pockets of teacher trainees coming here for informal discussions and late suppers. The place was known as "Congo Bar" mainly because the operator of the eating stall was an ex-soldier who served in Congo as a Malaysian United Nations representative under the International Red Cross.

This ex-soldier was a friendly guy and he used to join our tables now and then to narrate us his story of his experience in Congo. His stores were interesting to hear but since he had other customers to attend, he often could not finish telling his stores till the end. We made up the conclusions on our own. He was fun to talk to. We were his good and regular customers. His eating stall was located at a strategic spot catering for three educational institutes. It had my college, Technical Teacher Training College and the Alam Shah Secondary school encircling it.

In the evenings when most students were free this "Congo Bar" becomes a thriving activity area. We have had many an evening's here during our two year stay at the college with our menu of local Malay dishes. We also had the menu of laughter and jokes to cheer us always.

Though we had exams and assignments to complete we had no apparent fear of failing the papers. Our seniors have told us not to worry of any failures because it did not happen to them. It was the same for the year before that. There was an unspoken rule that the college will not fail students after spending so much money on the students. It was an unspoken rule that all will pass. This information was passed down to us. Due to this informal information we felt there is no pressure for us to pass the exams. Even the worst of us will pass the exams and exams were just show pieces for record purposes.

Honestly I do not know whether it was true or not but experiencing from my observations the trainee teachers generally were knowledgeable people. There were no reasons for us to fail the exams. The trainee teachers' general knowledge was fairly good. Most questions asked in the examination were general in nature. All the trainee teachers could answer the questions and I do not see any reasons as to why they would fail.

There is no pressure to pass the exams and we too had no fear towards it. I was told very much later by some reliable sources that the training was more towards preparing us to become good teachers. It was not their objective to have a scholarly type of teacher who only knows how to score good marks.

These non- existent fears made us very relaxed unlike life during the school days where our parents would be waiting at the doorsteps to demand for the results. More importantly was that, we did not have any pressure to do well in the exams. What was required unofficially was that we were participating in the college life holistically. Being participative as a teacher trainee was the ingredient used to pass us and make us to become a good teacher.

Besides the studies we were required to participate in games. I could not enter the football team because there were far better football players than me. However due to my robust size and eagerness to play rugby, I was selected into the college rugby team. As thus in inter -college competitions we had to participate as the college's representative. Interestingly we had to compete against sports club rugby teams and other college rugby teams. Though we had good players in our team we could not reach the pinnacle as a champion even though we played in the various competitions. It was always the story that the other teams were better than us. However I stand tall to remember that I played rugby for my college.

I also took part in athletics for short distance races. I was quite a fast runner in 100 meters and 200 meters distance. I represented the college many times in competitions when we were invited for athletics meets. Though during my tenure we never got any presents for individual events but as a team we had emerged as winners. Our relay team could tap the individual capabilities of each participant. It was always a proud day for me when we triumphed as a winner in the tournaments' we participated.

We had a healthy lifestyle in college. We had sumptuous breakfast, lunch and dinner in the college dining hall. Every day we had alternatives of fish and chicken, fish and mutton or beef. We hardly had any dishes catering for vegetarian people. They had to make do by choosing dishes that were vegetarian. In the dining Hall a crowd of about 500 student and lecturers can be seated at one time to relish on the food served.

Sometimes on formal occasions we all had to attire formally and be punctual. It was an atmosphere of grandeur and prestige. It was an honor for such grandeur and these occasions made us realize that we were meant for greater things and the country expected it from us. These grand dining were all over. I still miss those great days.

I was told that colleges' nowadays do not practice these types of colonial dinners in such grandiose presentations and pomp to have an impact on the diners. We have drifted to a lesser informal manner of dining. Dressing in formal attire for dining are now reminiscent episodes. We also had monthly dances where we got to dance the fox- trot and other popular dances. Via these dances we could get over the inhibitions of being shy.

We became more sociable and friendly towards each other. From a shy estate boy I have transformed to become a dynamic young teacher. However we were yet to master the fine decorum of being a fine English gentlemen civil servant type. The eloquence of the British regime has disappeared and the new informalities of the Malaysian culture were being practiced. The practices of the colonial past were forgotten and the present "care-free" attitude had seeped in to the fabrics of the Malaysian civil service and student culture.

Besides the formalities of learning and researching in our studying regime, the atmospheres at the college were the most unforgettable episode of my life. Those two years in college was a life of mirth, laughter and total joy. We did not have responsibilities towards our families nor towards the society made us very relaxed. Though there could be pockets of individuals who were dipped into sorrow or sadness the majority displayed happiness. Most of us seemed to be as problem free people. Rarely did we share stories of sadness or sorrow. Maybe it was the age we were oblivion to negative situations. We did not attract negativity into our lives. My group of about 12 to 14 students ware always happy and we had tons of jokes to share which made us to be care free.

From the time of waking up until the time we go to bed we could be sharing jokes and laughter. It was the way of our college life. We always had time to finish our assignments though we had to admit we did a lot of "cut and paste" methods by sharing and collaborating on the assignments. The lecturers were happy we completed their given tasks. I suspect they knew we copied or shared our resources. To them it was the learning that counts and they seldom made much fuss on our work. However there were times they made noise on the frequent delinquents who miss the classes or do not hand the assigned work on time. Fortunately my groups of friends were mostly punctual and prompt in doing our work. We participated well in our group activities and the lecturers knew our individual names. We enjoyed the classes by participating fully.

For us learning was fun and we enjoyed by participating. Sometimes activities that involved physical activity were abhorred by my friends and they tend to find ways and avenues to escape. I somehow was not like that because for me and most of my friends we enjoyed both the mental and the physical activities. For us, the stay in college was enjoyable and good and we seldom abused the freedom.

My college days were a real transition days for me. It was here that I learned respect and regards for my fellow classmates, fellow students, the lecturers and the system. I became a popular student and hence they elected me as a Treasurer for the Student's union. As a Union treasurer I collected RM 2.00 from each student and the money would be forwarded to me by the college office. At the end of the month I had to go to the bank to deposit the members' money into the College Union Account. As a treasurer I had new responsibilities. Need to keep the accounts in order and answer any queries. Interestingly it was here that I learned to write cheques and issued them as our mode of payments.

As a treasurer I used to get some side benefits to which I would categorize as gifts when I made the payments to the vendors' promptly. Bulk of the expenses was taken up by the college magazine and I need to liaise with the editorial board and the printers. It was fun having new responsibilities. These responsibilities entailed me with time management skills. Though I was not that busy but it was here that I learned how to categorize appointments and work schedules in relation to the position as a treasurer.

The two years of college life moved swiftly and we were hardly settled, the two year time period was up. We got our postings as teachers. All of us were scattered all over the country. I got Seremban as my posting to the Vocational School in Seremban. It was a brand new school and I was happy at the posting. My family had already moved from Taiping to Kuala Lumpur and thus over the weekends I can get to visit therm.

My college organized a farewell dinner for all of us and it was an emotional departure for many of us. Some of my friends were leaving behind their girl friends who were their juniors. My particular group was not focused into getting into any romantic relationships. We were not sad on that account but we became sad on the account that our laughter and jokes were coming to an end.

Two of our friends who were earlier in our inner circle but when they got entangled with girl friends at the second year of study, they drifted to become our outer circle. Though we were sad on this account, our lives have to move on. Until today we are yet to meet again for a reunion.

On the last day of our college life there were a lot of tears flowing from the girls. Though we men were holding on to the tears we were emotionally moved too. We realized the friendships and togetherness that bonded us was going to be ended. The best part of my life just flew away. We all departed with a heavy heart. College life was indeed interesting and it was a happy two years short journey.

Teaching life

Teaching had been a real bundle of joy for me but only until 1978. The medium of instruction changed to Bahasa Malaysia and my life changed. Prior to these, English was the main language used for most of the school activities. Everything moved using English. The staff meetings were conducted in English and English was the main stay language in all the secondary schools. Even Chinese schools emphasized on English. English has been the language introduced by the British colonial masters since the time of Penang Free School built in the year 1903. All the schools other than Malay, Chinese and Tamil vernacular primary schools used English as the medium of instruction. In those good old days the 'Senior Cambridge

Certificate' examinations were conducted here but the papers were marked in England. A pass in Senior Cambridge was a status qualification.

I stand tall to mention that I have qualified with a senior Cambridge qualification. My exam papers were marked in England and this qualification had a prestigious reputation in those days. Subsequently the Form five qualifications were renamed as "Sijil Pelajaran Malaysia (SPM) or the Malaysian Certificate of Education (MCE) and by this time all papers were marked locally in Malaysia. There was a slow decline of the English language. Its usage lost its prominence and in 1978 all schools were instructed to conduct their lessons in Bahasa Malaysia. English Language was retained as a language subject only. Over the years the quality and usage of the English language declined.

My dilemma as a teacher was for the commercial subjects whereby I had to teach, Commerce, Principles of Accounts, typewriting and other commercial subjects in the Malay language was a challenging effort. We were trained in the English language but we were required to use the Malay language as a medium of instruction. The transition caused me a lot of difficulties in trying to master a new language. However most of the commercial subjects used a lot of English words or terms in the Malay language. At least that was a small relief.

My first posting was in Seremban. I must narrate the pleasant feeling of me stepping my foot in Seremban. I felt very welcomed by the state of Negeri Sembilan. I was supposed to change buses at Seremban to visit my friend at Rantau. It was agreed that I put up at his house before I report for duty at the Vocational School in Ampangan, Seremban. When I stepped foot at Seremban, the taxi touts were plying for passengers by shouting Rantau, Mambau, Bahau and other places. These names sounded like my name Apparau (Apparow) and for a moment I was thinking they were calling for me. Infect I was wondering as to how they knew my name. I however realized that they were only plying for passengers.

My name was being called many times and I felt Negeri Sembilan was welcoming me to this new place. My stay in Seremban was very eventful and it was a joyous stay. My life in this school was good and fruitful too. It was here that I applied to do my Form Six via the Stamford College correspondence course. I realized that the graduate teachers were getting more pay than the college trained teachers for similar work duties, hence my decision to do Form Six was a good decision. This led me to continue my education and learning until I reached to obtain my doctorate.

The first day of my teaching life was interesting. I had no class to attend to. I was asked to be a class teacher for a Form IV class but the class was yet to arrive. It was January and being the beginning of the year my class was yet to be formed. My school only caters for Form IV and Form V students. Students after completing their Form III examinations would need to apply to enter Vocational Schools. They would be selected following a process of interviews conducted by the various Vocational schools throughout the country to determine their inclinations for the various vocational subjects being offered.

The interview board would need to determine and assess the appropriate students were being selected for the various courses that were being offered by the Vocational schools. They get to enter the Vocational system only from the months of late March or early Aprils in the year. As thus my class began only then. I had to wait for their arrival.

These processes were being practiced by all vocational schools throughout the country. It was implemented because only the right candidates' were chosen by the team of interviewers. The interview process filters and only enthusiastic students who prefer to follow their chosen vocations will be allowed to enter the vocational Stream of Education. Unlike the students from the normal Academic schools who can enter the gates of Public Universities, these students were trained to join the job market in the numerous factories' in Malaysia.

Malaysia needs many such talent and skill workers to be employed in the production lines of the various factories. However students who showed potential to better themselves, then the Polytechnic Colleges absorbed them for their various technical programs. From there they can pursue to degree levels in the universities. As thus students who entered the Vocational streams were not denied further education.

Meanwhile I was given some subjects to teach in the Form Five classes. I was aged 22 years when I began my teaching experience. The students were around 17 years old and there were not much age disparity between me and the students. They could accept me as their peers and were rather jovial and friendly towards me. I remember discussing in my first class the benefits of knowing the Principles of Accounting and the students' participations were very encouraging and good. I was indeed very happy at the dialogue session and instantly fell in love with my teaching job.

My two years in Seremban was short lived. I was reluctant to leave Seremban because my stay here was really enjoyable. I applied to be transferred to Kuala Lumpur or Klang. My family had just shifted from Taiping to Kuala Lumpur and they needed me to be in Kuala Lumpur with them.

I got my transfer and they posted me to Kapar, a suburb town of Klang. My stay here only lasted for two months because there was a transfer order for me to go to Kuala Selangor. The Ministry of Education considered this as a rural positing. It was a policy then that all teachers need to serve in rural areas for a short duration of time. I believe my transfer had nothing to do with the policy because someone wanted to be in Kapar and not in Kuala Selangor and for this person's convenience I was chosen for the transfer. I was angry and furious for being made use to favour the person at my expense. I was angry but what could I do. No use fighting the government machinery and after all I was a bachelor then. What was there to complain when I could always go back home over the weekends. At the same time my service in Kuala Selangor was considered as a rural posting. After this posting I need not serve anymore at a rural place.

I slowly relented for the transfer and in good tidings began to like the rural setting. Life here was interesting and colorful. The students were mostly from fishermen villages, rubber and oil palm plantations and the kampongs. Being rural the students were respectful towards the teachers. They were obedient and passive in their behavior. Though they were not as bright as the city children they however had a good attitude towards learning. They were eager to break free from the shackles of poverty and move up in life.

I spent three years in Kuala Selangor by renting a room on top of a tailor shop which was close to the school. I was punctual for my school duties and spent most afternoons coaching the boys into athletics and other related sports activities. Most of the men teachers could be found in the fields attending to the various sports activities. Football and hockey were our primary sports activities. Sometimes we got into the games as players when we do not have enough players at hand. The students being young could outpace us and snatch the football or the hockey ball from us. We have to face reality being not fit as the youngsters.

Besides the games we also coached the students on dramas. Shakespeare plays were being rehearsed and presented at the Annual Speech days. These events were being done in the late evenings around 7.30 till 9.00 pm. Those teachers who liked literature and arts did come in to assist the teachers who were assigned to coach the students.

I always had leanings towards literature and thus I was one of the regular teachers who could be seen in the school helping the students in their preparations at the rehearsals. I enjoyed participating in these activities. Debating competitions and elocution contests were regular annual features as a school activity. I was sometimes invited to be a judge or given the task to improve the student's arguments. These services were rendered with joy by me. Furthermore what else could I do in a rural setting when we seldom have own activities elsewhere.

Sunset watching was our regular activity. After having my shower and prior to dinner I usually adjourn to the jetty which is at the mouth of the Kuala Selangor River. It is from this jetty that people from Kuala Selangor would take the ferry to go over to the other side of the river to Pasir Panjang, Tanjung

Karang and Sekinchan. Most of the outstation teachers and the government officials who were posted here gather at the jetty to watch the suns' setting.

The horizon was noticeable from here and with the meeting of the river water to the sea and the setting of the sun makes it a scenic sight to watch. It was also good place to gather in the evenings. We exchanged stories of the days or any other mundane matters that concerned us. As the evenings turn to dusk, our groupings then adjourned to the dinner tables provided by the various restaurants.

We had about three restaurants in Kuala Selangor that we could go to have a decent meal. When we have a crowd of about eight or ten people we opened a table. We then place our orders to our likings. One particular dish that evolved through our combinations which we ordered the cook at our regular restaurant was called the "Chegu punya" dish. This dish was concocted by the teachers plying the restaurant. This particular dish gained popularity and became a mainstay dish for the restaurant. The other groups also liked this dish and place the order for this dish by calling it "Chegu punya" and the restaurant cook knew this dish.

I was told that the dish became a popular menu for the restaurant. The local people from Kuala Selangor also ordered this particular dish whenever they dine at this restaurant. My friend who visited this restaurant after a few years was surprised when a group of policemen were ordering the "chegu punya" dish for their dinner. He later asked the restaurant owner as to the popularity of the "chegu punya" dish and the reply he got was that this particular dish was his trademark dish. According to him many customers' throng the restaurant mainly for this dish. He sounded happy that this was his pride dish to offer to his customer. We were happy that we have left behind a legacy in the form a culinary dish for the local folks. I wonder whether the dish is still being offered now.

My stay at Sekolah Sultan Abdul Aziz Shah were for the years 1975, 1976 and 1977 which took me to a period of enjoyable teaching experience. The three years stay here was good. The parents were good to us and sometimes they sent their bounty fish catches to our dinner tables to express their gratitude. The students were respectful and obedient to the teachers. When the students heard that I was being transferred to another school in Klang they protested but when they came to know that the transfer was due to my own request they reluctantly let me go.

In 1978, I was asked to report duty at a brand new school. Due to my earlier experience at Sekolah Menegah Vokasional in Seremban, the Ministry of Education felt I was appropriate to serve at Sekolah Menegah Vokasional School, Klang. Since this school was a new school only Form Four students would be offered places here. In the following year 1979 we had both Form Four and Form Five in full operations.

We had about 45 teachers teaching the various subjects. The school population reached about 800 students in total. Compared to academic schools our student populations at vocational schools were always lower. We only catered for Forms fours and fives unlike the academic schools that catered for Forms one, two, three, four and five. Some academic schools also offered Form Six classes.

My sojourn at Sekolah Menengah Vokasional, Klang was from the years 1978 until 2006. It was a long 28 years here. I could last this long in this school was mainly due to the fact that I enjoyed teaching here too. A group of teachers who were trained to teach commercial subjects were placed into the Commerce Department. There were five of us to teach various commercial subjects. I was asked to teach Principles of Accounts for all classes.

In the early years at this school I had a hard time converting myself to teach my subjects in Bahasa Malaysia. Earlier it was thought in English. 1978 was the year chosen to implement all subjects to be thought in Malay. The English language was retained as a subject in the curriculum. It was not easy adapting to Bahasa Malaysia which was a new language for me. However it being the national language for the country we were willing to learn and adopt this into our teaching duties.

Though I had a hard time picking up the language of the country, it was a joy too to learn the rudiments of the grammar were applied over the lingua of Bahasa Malaysia or rather the national language of the country. The students had a roaring time of laughter as they realized that I was getting the prefixes mixed up. In the Malay language the usage of prefixes determine the meanings of the word. One such error I made when the students thundered with their laughter was when I told them I will show them my sexual organ when I actually wanted to mean that I was feeling ashamed being their class teacher. In the Malay language being ashamed is represented by the word "malu" and when the prefix "kemaluan" is used it means to express the sexual organ. When I narrated the matter to my teacher friends at the staff room they too started laughing at my usage of the word. Then they told me that when I used the word "kemaluan" it meant to express that I was willing to display my sexual organ.

I realized that this Malay language is a delicate language and it needs extensive care to use the words diligently. Though I was conscious with the usage of the words but in due time with the courage to make mistakes I slowly leaned the language well. Within a period of about two years I became comfortable with the usage of the Malay language. Within a short span of time gap, I became good using the Malay language. Its usage was instrumental for the teaching of Principles of accounts in the country. It was trying periods and I became quite an authority in the usage of the Malay language to pen a book entitled "Ulangkaji Prinsip Perakaunan (Revision of the Principles of Accounts)–" for Form four students.

The usage of the Malay language became prominent and official for all subjects in the school curriculum. Eventually all schools were required to use the Malay language in all subjects except for the English language which remained as a subject. The damage that happened was that the students became good with the usage of the Malay language but the quality of the English language floundered and became weak.

The standard of the English language declined very much and we as teachers could not do much. It was being the policy of the then political government that the English language was not an important factor. The government wanted its own identity with the Malay language.

However some parents realized that the usage of English language will always remain prominent and useful. These parents turned to be correct because their children could find entries into twinning programs in private universities and pursue their tertiary education.

The Malaysian Education System was at confusion paths when they had two streams of education systems. The normal schools followed the normal academic path and the other stream offered technical and vocational studies. These two systems were a parallel system of education for students leaving the Form Three's. The technical and vocational paths were designed for students who wanted to pursue engineering programs.

Technical Education was meant for the brighter students who could pursue engineering programs via the polytechnic colleges and the vocational system was meant for students who did not excel in their Form Three public examinations. The vocational students could pick on skills that were useful for factory works or jobs that require handy skills. These students were meant for the needs of the various factories that could improve their production capacity.

There was a paradigm shift in the political thinking that these vocational students could also be upgraded to join the technical streams. In reality the government felt that the vocational education system was more expensive to maintain and thus the shift of all vocational schools to be streamlined as technical schools. Due to this revised pattern the vocational school where I thought was changed to become a technical school. It was renamed as Sekolah Menengah Teknik, Klang.

Life at Sekolah Menegah Teknik was more or less the same. However the environment at the school has now changed due to the improved status of the school. Students felt their reputations were now upgraded being students of Technical schools. Some of the subjects were upgraded to suit the nature of the technical system. The subjects were more theory based and less of practical training approach. Using this approach saved the government a lot of money in reducing its expenditure. They need not provide the equipments for the practical training. The paradigm shift was to transfer the costs of training to the respective factories or the private sectors to provide them the practical trainings when they join them as employees.

In this new system of technical education my job scope had me to teach another interesting subject called as "Pendidikan Moral" or Moral Education to the non-Malay students. Interestingly this subject was an examination subject and many students could not score well and teachers were reluctant to take on this subject.

I took on this subject because I wanted a change from teaching Principles of Accounts and an opportunity to teach a different subject. Furthermore I quite liked the topics of morality and religion. The number of students who took this subject was few. The non Malays were required to take 'Pendidikan Moral' and the Malays were required to take 'Agama'.

I used an interactive method to teach 'Pendidikan Moral' I made the students to prepare and present their view on the various topics and marks were awarded on the presentations skills and there were no penalties imposed upon them when they went out of topic. This provided the impetus for the students to make their own research and kindle the interest on the various topics. We discussed on the rights and wrongs of the various moral topics. Probably this approach brought in new enthusiasm on the students and their score ratings turned good.

I had a good 100 % passes in the SPM (Sijil Pelajaran Malaysia) examination. Quite immediately I became the talk of the town and the news spread that Sekolah Menegah Teknik scored 100

% passes on this difficult subject called as Pendidikan Moral. Other schools began to invite me to give a preparatory talk to their students as to how to score on this subject. I willingly obliged them for wanting to be generous in sharing knowledge.

Though I detested the change in the medium of instructions in the year 1978 onwards, I realized that the usage of the Malay language was a necessity for the sake of a common identity amongst all the races in Malaysia. Over the due period I became quite fluent in the usage of the Malay language and began to enjoy cracking jokes with the students. I am quite friendly with the students and they too reciprocate my love and kindness. My fear of making grammatical mistakes vanished and since I myself becoming familiar with the Malay language usage became bolder and bolder to use it to disseminate information in teaching my subjects. I apparently became the "Cikgu" for them.

In due time, I looked forward to do my teaching duties and eager to make my students score in the respective subjects tutelage by me. I made sure that I finished the syllabus in time and have prepared them well to confront their public examinations well. I gave them enough homework exercises and have encouraged them to copy from their friends if their work is undone. I just did not want to hear of any excuse if the homework undone. My rationale is that whilst copying they still lean and it is better than not doing at all. As thus my students have a common understanding of my modus operandi that my work must be done and that there is no compromise for undone work.

I was fortunate in getting my students comply with my requirements and the only reason I attribute for getting their cooperation was due to the fact that they do respect me as their teacher and that I do mean business with sincerity for their welfare at heart. Probably due to these common understanding my students results were always on the top ranking. However failures do arise amongst the students but then it was beyond my own redemptions. Failures do happen and that were some of my pitfalls as a normal teacher.

I had an uncanny ability in getting the students to cooperate with me. I encourage the students to learn by discussing and quite immediately after teaching them a hard point I encourage them to do exercises and getting the problem solved. I allow them to discuss and arrive at the solution. Class participation by the students makes learning interesting. I will get the students who solved a particular accounting problem from the various exercises provided to come forward and explain to the class as to how he derived to the answer.

In my years of teaching I found this method of teaching very interesting for both the students and myself. We enjoyed the discussions that ensued in the arguments as to how the various accounting questions were answered objectively with understanding. In due time my students scored well in the public examinations. My reputation as an accounts teacher increased. I managed to obtain consistent good grades from the students. The news spread fast and I indeed became a popular Accounts teacher in my Klang District. Due to this added fame I normally was invited by many of the schools in the Klang District to give a motivational talk to their students. At the same time the students were shown the basics of how to score well in 'Principles of Accounts' as a subject.

Due to my popularity as an accounts teacher, a popular book publisher approached me to write a text book to cater for the

Principles of Accounts subject that would be used by the Form four students. My book was not marketed as an authorized text book but was sold as a Revision book for Principles of Accounts. I was told by the publisher that my book was widely used by most schools throughout Malaysia and the teachers used my book to teach. They did not use the official text book approved by the Ministry of Education.

The following year the publisher approached me to write another book for Form Five students as a continuation but I refused. I refused mainly because I realized the publisher has shortchanged me at the payments for the full royalty payments.

In the same year I was approached by another publisher to write the book for both Form Four and Five combined and they extracted a contract from me to write only exclusively for them only. I duly wrote the book for them and they too made their payments as agreed but however the printing of the book never materialized due to some issues by the new publisher. As thus my Principles of Accounts book for Form four had a short lifecycle because the market preferred a combined book for both Forms four and five together. My book's life cycle only lasted for a period of about three years only.

However there was a change in the syllabus and thus new books need to replace the old versions.

Other publishers were more dynamic in getting their books printed and flooding the schools with their books. Over time my book was already replaced and forgotten. This was however a very enriching experience for me and gave me an opportunity to have a book published under my name.

My life as a teacher was interesting but the salary was never enough for me to sustain my family with good providence. Every time an expense incurred I had to stretch my money to meet the expenses. Many of my teacher friends were involved in part time jobs to earn second incomes to meet the expanding expenses of their family. I did not involve myself into securing second income opportunities. The cash constraints got me and my family members to live frugally with minimal expenses. This strategy helped me to pull my family through to sustain and grow as a family unit. My children learned responsibility by learning to live frugally.

Conducting school sports is an annual sports activity was quite a joy to many teachers and students. For the students it takes them away from the mundane work of studying. For the teachers it was a necessary break away from their teaching duties.

An air of festivity takes over in the name of competition. Students and teachers were given respective 'school houses'. Selection or groupings were done randomly and thus in the name of sports there were few complaints in the method of choosing. According to the school calendar everyone in the school would be aware at to the priorities and things that need to be done by the respective houses. Selection of office bearers for the respective houses would have been done and these office bearers delegate the various duties to their sports house mates.

The sports practices are done in the evenings at the school compound. Various teachers who had their respective duties earmarked would be present to ensure the activities were being carried out. Much fun and joy were being shared amongst the students and the teachers. Healthy simple competitions abound at the practices.

Along with the sports practices, competitions were held to keep the winners and remove the losers via the practice of "Sports Heats". In these Heats all the respective house representatives are asked to participate and run. The purpose was to weed out the slow runners and retain the fast runners. Sometimes we have "Heats 2" to further weed out the slower runners from the champions. The real intent was to have only the finalists performing on the real sports days.

From these activities, marks or points are awarded to the respective houses and that promotes the competitor environments and the friendly battle begins. It was during this period we can witness the fierce struggle being put in by the students to excel and win a trophy for their respective sports houses. In this struggle the teachers too join in the fun and this adds to the competition. Sometimes the headmaster or rather the principal shows favoritism inadvertently due to someone close to him. When that happens, the students belonging to other houses will put up a row condemning the action of the headmaster. However the whole episode is taken in good spirits by all.

During these periods of annual sports activities and the annual cross country sports activities, the atmosphere at the school transforms into a buzz of activity. The annual cross countries were normally held a bit earlier in the months of February and sports were held in the months of April. I, being a lover of sports, participate happily in these activities and enjoy performing the tasks allocated to every one of us. It was during these periods that the schools experience an environment of festivity. After the sports the school begins to focus on academic pursuits.

Besides the annual school sports we also host an annual "Speech Day" to celebrate the success of the students achievements in the field of academics. We invite the parents to witness the grand day meant for their children. We also invite special important guest for the function to add value for the function. For this function we also involved students to present their works via exhibitions and other portrayals. Some of our students get involved in staging a performance for the invited guests. These functions also involved us for the preparations to make the occasion grand and presentable.

These two annual occasions are our formal activities every year and at the end of the year the students were being prepared for the final examinations. Coaching and guiding the students to excel in their examinations would then become our focus for the students. These periods around we have night classes or weekend classes to prepare the students better for them to perform better in their examinations.

Over the years I had been busy doing the daily chores and performing the allocated tasks assigned to me. It made me realize that the time for retirement was up. I was given an option to retire at a later period of 56 years but I chose to retire at the age of 55.

On my 55th birthday the school arranged for my retirement day in a grand way. They wanted to convey their gratefulness to me for serving the school 28 long years. In the morning they arranged for a school assembly and all the teachers and the students were gathered. Respective students' from various classes to whom I taught were chosen to speak a few words to thank me. Some teachers too took the occasion to speak about me and my contribution towards the school. On behalf of the school my headmaster/principal spoke and conveyed his appreciation towards my 28 years of service to the school in various activities.

At the end I was asked to speak. I gave an inspiring speech to the students and gave them some piece of good advice.

I also prepared a short poem to describe my life at the school. It was entitled as:

Life Journey in Sekolah Menengah Teknik

I came to you when you were born in 1978
As a baby I was there to cuddle you
I held you as a dear child
Nurtured and partook into all your activities.

Oh! Dear, time really moved from seconds to minutes,
Minutes to hours, hours to days and days to weeks,
Weeks to months and months to years
And now you are a strong young man of 28 years.

I loved you well and you loved me well too
For the years of love with you
Will tell the tale of our bonding and fraternity
For together we braved all these 28 years.

You started as a Vocational school
But now you have upgraded yourself to
become Sekolah Menegah Teknik
To become the talk of the town as the
best school after Kolej Islam

You have seen five headmasters and now
you have a sixth headmaster
Who has a doctorate degree to take care of you.

You were then surrounded by oil palm plantations
You had no neighbors and you were the only solitary building
We can see the progress you have brought to Bayu Perdana
And now you have new young neighbors too.

Many students have passed by us
Together we have steered them to greater heights
I stop here, but you will continue to
see more students to come by
And be proud that they came under
your roof for their alma mater

Thus my young man, Sekolah Menengah Teknik
I can only have sweet memories of you dear
With grace of god I bid you goodbye adieu
To leave you in the hands of my able friends

Myself (Apparow Sannasai)

At the end of the speech all the students and the teachers applauded my inspiring speech. It was a good speech and I could see some of the students were in tears. After the speech I was showered with many gifts from various in-house school organizations and departments as a farewell gift for my services at the school.

The students lined up at the roadside to wave be me good bye. I was driven out by a special pre-arranged land rover and my job was to stand up and wave them good bye as I as driven out of the school. My car was left outside the school compound from which I was allowed to drive home. I bid my last good bye to the school that endeared my 28 years of my love for teaching.

As I was driving home knowing it would be my last journey home from the school I cherished and loved. A sense of sorrow enveloped me. Tears developed around my eyes but knowing that it was my birthday and that this was my retirement day, I accepted the fact that life must go on. So be it.

Pursuing ICSA (the first degree), MBA and PHD

I ventured to study HSC (Higher School Certificate) part time by subscribing to Stamford College Correspondence program. I followed the lessons in the correspondence program diligently and sent the answered assignments dutifully. It was a difficult due to constraints on time. Marking student's exercise books took away a lot of my time and did not have much time to spare for self study. However decisions are being made and money already paid for the correspondence course.

The lessons presented in the correspondence course were good and self explanatory and could understand the contents of the lessons. At the end of each lesson there were two types of exercises. The first type was questions meant for self analysis and it serves as a revision for the contents displayed in the lesson. The second sets of questions are to be answered diligently and then sent to the Stamford College for marking and evaluation. The questions were grueling and it was never easy to answer the questions immediately. The questions were designed in a way that we have to understand the subject content thoroughly before they could be answered. Reference was allowed to answer the questions and they allowed hand writing work to be sent. Sometimes the tutors preferred type written scripts to be sent mainly because they could not decipher our writings. I sent hand written scripts for marking.

I enrolled for Economics, History, Bahasa Malaysia, English Literature and General Paper. I realized that the quality standard for Higher School Certificate (HSC) was quite high unlike the Ordinary School Certificate (SC). I realized that additional efforts need to put in to master the subjects. In the first attempt I obtained two principals and three subsidiaries which gave me for a full certificate but however my principal passes were weak. The passes were insufficient to provide me the qualification to enter Malaysian public universities.

I made another new attempt to do well in the examination the following year. This time around I managed to obtain three principals and they were strong principals. I did qualify for the university entry and was eligible to be registered as a student. I was delighted and happy but however this providence was short lived because the university told me that I still could not qualify due to the fact that I did not have a credit in Bahasa Malaysia in Sijil Pelajaran Malaysia.

I told the authorities that I have a pass in Bahasa Malaysia in Sijil Pelajaran Malaysia (SPM) and a principal pass in Bahasa Malaysia at the Higher School Certificate (HSC). I reminded them that it was an acceptable qualification at the Ministry of Education for me to continue as a teacher. At this particular period all government institutions were insistent upon a credit in Bahasa Malaysia and as a result the university turned down my application. They were adamant that an applicant should have a credit in Bahasa Malaysia at the Malaysian School Certificate level. My teaching job was an exception to the rule because I became a teacher before this rule was implemented. My entry to the university was not successful. I became very disappointed and sad. This was a case of so near and yet so far.

During these periods of despair and not knowing what to do next, that I met a lawyer friend at a function. As we were discussing my unsuccessful entry to the university he pointed to me a way out. He suggested that I take up professional management programs instead. He mentioned that these can be studied on own provided that I can become a member of the professional body. It just requires preparing and participating in their examinations.

I had two options. The first option was to sit for ACCA (Association of Certified and Chartered Accountants) and the next was to enroll for ICSA (Institute of Chartered Secretaries & Administrators. I chose the second option and quickly made the application to register as a student at the famed Institute of Chartered Secretaries and Administrators, London, United Kingdom. My application was accepted and I became happy again. Now I am in the pursuit for higher education. I notified my employer of new status as a part- time student. It was mandatory that I inform them and I duly informed the Ministry of Education who was my employer.

I found this program as very interesting. I was provided the syllabus and the exam dates. The examinations were to be held at the British Council in Kuala Lumpur. Enthusiastically I bought the appropriate books and made my study plan to meet these new challenges. Had to juggle my work time, play time and study time accordingly. The examinations were held every six months and I had to complete eight modules. Each module consisted of two subjects and it was required to pass the two subjects for consideration as a clearance of one module. Studying for one module or two subjects for six months was very appropriate for me. I found that I could also spend time for work and study with not much burden.

There were times I became ambitious when I attempted to sit for two modules at one time. This turned out to be disastrous because I happened to pass two subjects but in different modules. As a result of this folly I need to re-sit both the modules. In one attempt I even sat for three modules at one attempt thinking that the earlier modules were only revision subjects for me. Luckily for me I managed to clear two modules at that particular sitting. Studying for more modules caused me more stress. I could not focus well simultaneously on the teaching job and the studies. I found it was wiser to clear one module each time. I applied this study plan and eventually cleared it over a period of five and a half year. Upon completion I was awarded graduate ship as a Chartered Secretary and Administrator member of the prestigious Institute of Chartered Secretaries and Administrators, London, United Kingdom.

I graduated ICSA (Institute of Chartered Secretaries & Administrators) in 1983 and this qualification was recognized as a degree at my work place by the Ministry of Education, Malaysia. Due to this qualification I was conferred as a graduate teacher which provided me a pay rise. If only I had not left school in 1969 and had continued to the university I could have been a graduate in the year 1973. Instead I became a graduate in 1983. I was behind time for ten long years. As the saying goes it is better late than never applies to me.

I was coaxed to apply for an administrative job at the private sectors. During the period of 1983's there was a general recession in Malaysia and much managerial jobs were not available then. Firms were retrenching their workers or downsizing them. Since I enjoyed teaching the commercial subjects and was already conferred into the graduate scale I felt it was better to remain as a teacher experiencing job security. I remained a teacher until the day I retired in June 2006.

I went for an education fair in Kuala Lumpur and got enticed into attending a talk given by Dr John Ross from Durham University, United Kingdom. He was mentioning the availability of Distance Learning Program that could be done from the comforts of the home. He mentioned the ratio of worked assignments and marks allocated for the examinations. The examinations would be done at the British Council annually. A Malaysian representative was available to help and guide the Malaysian students. He also mentioned that the University caters for international s students and that students were from all over the world. We would be the first batch from Malaysia. The University was promoting 'Distance Learning' and was recruiting international students from all over the world. The "Distance Learning Method" was also new for them.

I inquired as to the status of my ICSA being used as the entry qualifications for the Masters in Business Administration (MBA) at University of Durham, United Kingdom. Green light was given by them and with that I made preparations to enroll as a student at this prestigious university from United Kingdom. I heard this was the third oldest university in United Kingdom and it was ranked amongst the top14[th].

I came and announced to my family in relation to the intention to do my Masters. My wife was very supportive and encouraging. My mother on the other hand was not too encouraging because she remembered my struggles for my HSC and ICSA. She knew that I would not have much time for family affairs. Though she was reluctant she knew the value of education and consented in the end. She knew studying would keep me home bound.

Quite immediately I retrieved my ambition to continue studying and obtain an MBA qualification from University of Durham which was a prestigious university. Paid the deposits for the course fee and embarked upon this study pursuit with enthusiasm. I knew the study schedule could take a toll on me because I had to juggle my work hours, family commitments and studying. Since I was enthusiastic and resolved to go through and be focused to obtain the MBA. I looked upon MBA as a prized trophy to be acquired.

The Malaysian representative who was the facilitator made some efforts to group all the students who have signed up for the programs. Fourteen of us gathered and narrated our reasons for joining the program. It was quite a good crowd and instantly we knew we could group together for self study. Some of the fellow MBA students were successful individuals on their respective businesses. They took turns to buy us lunch on the Sundays whenever we met for group discussions.

I realized that this MBA program would be instrumental for networking. Networkings were essential for business success and exchange of notes. I knew this MBA program will change my paradigm shift from being small minded to become more open minded. It was essential for new and bigger scopes. My thinking changed and I had to become magnanimous. I changed for the better.

We gathered on weekends to discuss some difficult topics and find solutions to answer the assignment questions. We felt the gathering was stimulating and it did help us to answer the questions. Everyone contributed in the discussion and they threw their own work experience to highlight the managerial issues in relation to the question assigned. All of us felt the group discussion was doing us good and we decided to maintain the study group. At one instance all of us were weak to understand Statistics under the subject Quantity Analysis. We engaged a university professor to coach us on the basics. We however rode on him to help us answer the assigned questions. We shared the tutoring costs and it was a beneficial exercise for all of us.

The discussion group dwindled and as we progressed to Parts 2, 3 and 4 our paces changed. Some were faster than the others. Some were natural drop outs and did not continue the pursuit citing excuses. I continued persistently but got delayed two times. At one time my mother demised during the crucial period of the examinations and I did not attempt to sit for the papers. The university only allowed two sittings per paper and it was wiser to avoid. At another period I had insufficient funds to pay the fees for the last stage 4. My commitments were heavy and could not source for any loans to pay up the fees. I had to let go for that particular year. The last part whereby we had to write a dissertation paper on a topic took me another year. All in all it took me a long 7 ½ years to complete my MBA program.

Invitation to receive the scroll at the Durham University campus could not be attended due to lack of funds in incurring the expenses for the flight tickets and lodgings. My earlier trip to the university campus when we were at stage 2 with my fellow course mates was sufficient to know the University environment. We were required to attend the residential program for two weeks. I took a bank loan when I was at stage 2 to pay for the trip to the University was yet to be settled at that time. I basically could not afford the trip to collect the scroll. Some of my friends, who could afford, attended the convocation ceremony. They reported that it was a grand affair indeed and that we missed the glory of receiving the scroll from a University that had a world standing ranking. In the year 2000 when I rightly qualified for the Durham MBA the university was ranked as the 13th in the United Kingdom. Sometimes life is like that. It reminds me to the parable of "So near and yet so far".

Though my MBA program from the Durham University was a distance learning program I never felt that I was separated from the university campus. The university included us into their programs and kept us informed of the activities that were transpiring at the main campus. Now and then representatives from the University would come by to meet the students. Some of them were visiting professors and they do present papers for some respected organizations. We as students were informed of their presence and we made earnest attempts to meet them at the hotels where they stay or attend the talks offered to us at a discounted price. We attended because it was an occasion for us to meet up with the professors and fellow MBA friends.

The university has now included us into their alumni body and do keep us informed of the various activities that abound at the campus. We are always welcomed and the university had made requests for us to donate. Some of the successful friends have donated generously and being a teacher I could not do so. Felt guilty many times for not being able to donate. What to do. This follows the classical saying that the spirit was willing but the flesh was failing.

Obtaining the degree for my MBA from Durham University make me feel proud and I do feel tall that I have acquired a degree from this prestigious university. I know Durham University was prestigious because when I applied to do my PhD at the University of Malaya, I was immediately accepted into the PhD program because of the Durham status. Friends in United Kingdom told me that it was difficult for their British locals to enter the university. It was the third oldest university after Cambridge and Oxford and its ranking was quite similar to these universities. The locals' looked upon Durham University as an elite university. We were lucky to be accepted into its fold.

The quality of its education was of high standards and it was not easy to pass its stringent standards. We have to score 80 % for the written papers and only awarded 10 % marks for each assignment and we have two assignments for each paper to answer. In order to pass, we still need 30 % marks to obtain from the examination paper in an event we could obtain perfect 20 % from the assignments. 50 % was the passing marks allocated by the University and each student was only allowed two re-sits for each paper. It was impossible to obtain passing marks from the university without knowing the content of the subject. Even when we attempted to answer the assignment questions we had to cover extensive research to answer the question. The assignments were mind stimulating and of a good quality. The marking standards at the university were high and only those students who presented quality answers could pass their respective papers. I do feel confident knowing that I had passed these papers from the University. Feel proud indeed to realize that I am a product of the Durham University in the year 2000 after seven years into this program.

After obtaining MBA and in the year 2001, I applied to get optional retirement from my teaching career. However my employer, the Ministry of Education rejected my application citing that there were not enough Accounting teachers in the Teaching Service. I had no choice but to continue my teaching job. Someone infused the idea into me why not pursue PhD. I was thinking why not?

Quite immediately I made approaches with University Malaya to pursue PhD. The university was very receptive towards my application and they asked me to present a small paper on the area of my interest. At this particular juncture of my life I was teaching Moral studies for a group if Non-Malay students in the school. I was attracted towards morals and ethics. There were times I have got angry at businesses that were unethical in their business practice. I do believe that businesses could follow the moral or ethical path and yet make profits. Since the university wanted me to explore on areas related to business I was thinking it could be a good research area. I prepared a small paper on ethics and values in Malaysian Business firms.

I was happy when the university contacted me to announce that I was selected for their PhD program and that they have assigned one professor to supervise and guide me for my research pursuit. I duly paid the monies for the registration and contacted the professor for an appointment. On the agreed date I met up with the professor and he was much younger than me. He is a pleasant person and very approachable. I liked him and knew he could help me with the research. He asked me as to the areas of business research which could interest me. I explained to him that I was interested in doing research for small businesses. I wanted to explore on Break Even analysis or anything that is focused towards ethics or business values.

We discussed and he agreed that we could try on 'business values' as to be my research area. He however agreed that I could confine my research towards small business firms. He advised me to read as many academic journals as possible in relation to small business firms and business values. He gave me another appointment date a month away. Meanwhile he wanted me to attend the some courses assigned by the university to attend. I had to attend five different courses and was required to pass these subjects. The five courses are: Research Methodology, Data Analysis, Management Information, Ethics and Small Business Management.

I could follow most of the courses but I had some difficulties in understanding Data Analysis. However my course mates were quite helpful in explaining the elements in relation to the analysis. I failed in the first instance of sitting for the examination. The professor was kind to allow me for a re-sit for this paper. I worked hard to clear this and was fortunate to obtain a clearance pass for this paper when I sat for the paper the second time. Within the first three semesters we were supposed to clear the course papers and then we were supposed to focus on the literature gathering and prepare the research methodology for my thesis paper.

Studying for my PhD was interesting because I was always juggling for time. Preparing lessons and handling student matters in school was occupying my time. At home I became glued to the personal computer extracting articles for my thesis. I was not so familiar to reading articles from the computer screen and hence I printed the articles. I have collected tons of these printed articles. Later I became a bit better with the usage of the computer. I learned to save these articles for reference at a later stage.

Using the personal computers was a transition and a big learning curve for me. I was from the generation where we used typewriters and I had to learn and use the personal computer. However over time things fell into place and I became adapt to the changes. The focus was to download enough articles and prepare the literature necessary for the research paper I proposed to do. Time moved fast and soon seven years had passed. Meanwhile my supervisor left the university and the University offered me a new supervisor to guide me. I could not accept the new supervisor because I was afraid he or she will request me to make changes and I was not prepared to do so. I felt my thesis was ready for the viva test.

My test came when I had to defend my thesis entitled "Impact of Ethical Business Values in Malaysian Firms". The viva went well but however the examiners were quiet. They probably did not raise many questions for me to answer because they respected my age. They told me to wait outside for them to determine my status. After some time they told me to enter the room and they broke the sad news that I have failed. According to them my research methodology was flawed and not appropriate for the study. I was stunned with the results. I could not accept the results but their comments were final and conclusive. I failed my Viva.

Requests for me to redo was not allowed because it was the policy of the university that I either pass or fail the viva test. In my case it was a major error due to the wrong methodology used. I knew the examiners and they respected me being a senior citizen. I was many years older than the examiners. I knew them personally. There must have been a major error in my thesis that the examiners had no choice but to fail me. They felt sorry for me.

I went into depression on this account. I could not face my children and family members because my ego was shattered. How could I, being popular accounts teacher fail a Viva-Test. I could not face my friends and the society. The news travelled fast and there were many inquiries. My ex- students came to know about my failure. Though they did not ridicule me I felt humiliated and could not accept the failure. After some time the truth settled on me that the thesis was really flawed and it was the correct reason for my failure. I began to accept that the research methodology used was wrong.

I was wallowing myself into a sorrow ball and was avoiding everyone. My family members became worried for my welfare. I assured them that I was alright and that I just need some time to recover. I found the space for inner silence was relieving. The silence period brought my senses to alive and I started asking myself what was that I was trying to proof. Failing a PhD paper was not a big deal. So what was wrong with failing? I only failed because of a wrong approach in the methodology. It did not prove that I was stupid but on the contrary the PhD journey has made me into a better person. I was a far much better person who at my age was still trying to pursue an academic qualification after retiring.

During the Literature Review writing I realized that businesses can still be practiced using ethical business values. I realized then that there're are business men who were very successful using good business values in their business operations. They were not only being successful but also have donated immensely. Their charity was from their business success. Though I could not prove empirically I knew at heart that I was correct. That sufficed me.

My friend Associate Professor Dr. Jeyaraman who was lecturing at the LimKokWing University at the business faculty got the winds that I was idling myself at home with a depression bout. He called me and requested me to redo the topic at the university. In the beginning I was reluctant and call it a day for educational pursuits. He did not allow me to sit and cry. He insisted and even offered to pay the fees. My family members too encouraged me. My son and daughter provided me good inspirations. They told me that if I did not pursue the new opportunity I would become a grumpy old man. I never wanted to be a grumpy man and I detest such men. My elder brother was one and that frightened me.

With new enthusiasm thrown at me, I approached my friend at the LimKokWing University. I told him that I intend to change my topic and do something closer to my heart. I wanted to venture on small businesses owned by Malaysian Indians. I requested Dr. Jeyaraman to be my supervisor and he agreed because he was familiar with my topic. As usual I was requested to write in my proposal paper for this new topic and submit for the senate's approval. I was duly registered as a new PhD student and was welcomed to purse my new pursuit.

The university approved my friend to be my supervisor. It was good for me because he highlighted me what are the areas for me to focus for the literature collection. My previous experience from University Malaya helped me to be independent but however I still met my friend to guide me. He was happy with my approach and requested me to continue gathering much literature.

As I was progressing in my research work I got the bad news that my friend had applied to join another university with added responsibilities and better pay. However he did not leave me on the lurch and he introduced me to Dr Ilham Sentosa to be my new supervisor. I had no choice because I need to seek supervisors (lecturers) who were from the university itself.

Dr. Ilham Sentosa was very supportive and he prepared a stringent timetable that I had to see him every fortnightly for two hours each. I have to brief him and show him my progress. He too was very supportive and guiding. We became friends but however the relationship of a teacher and a student remained. With his systematic guidance and supervision I was ready to submit my PhD work within a short span of 4 ½ years for the viva test.

The title of my new thesis was, "Determine the Critical Success Factors in Malaysian Indian firms and its contributions towards business performance". At the viva test the examiners were happy with my work but they asked me to trim my work and have only

9 hypotheses tested. My work had 45 hypotheses tested. They awarded me a pass with the corrections to be submitted within a period of three months period grace. I was overwhelmed with the pass and it was like a dream come true. I quickly rectified my thesis and resubmitted for the senate's approval. The internal examiner appointed by the university saw that I have done the necessary corrections and he gave his signature to the effect that I was awarded the PhD degree which was eluding me for years.

All in all the pursuit for PhD has taken me a long period of twelve years. MBA has taken in seven and half years. My attempt at first degree has taken me five and half years. The Form Six examination (Higher School Certificate – HSC) took me three years. It took me a long period of twenty eight years of part time study to achieve a dream that I envisioned to have when I was in school.

I earnestly thanked my supervisor, Dr. Ilham Sentosa, Dr. Jeyaraman, Dr. Batumalai, Dr. Arasan, Dr. Balachander Guru, Dr. Karuthen, Dr. Wan Sabri, Professor Dr. Mahendran, Professor Dr. Ainin and many other academicians who were instrumental for my final emancipation to get the elusive PhD degree. Professor Emeritus Dr. Lim Kok Wing himself congratulated me personally for my persistence in pursuing the alma mater. Receiving the scroll on the convocation day from the Pahang Sultana was the pinnacle for my achievements. Felt very settled and extremely happy. I could now rest

My daughter, son and wife were beaming with joy and tears when they witnessed their father and husband getting the scroll. To them I was a success and a source for their inspiration. They were happy that I was happy. My son told me privately that I will never be a grumpy old man.

It was the success at achieving the PhD qualification after twenty eight long years of patiently studying part- time that inspired me to write this book. I want to encourage others to study too. I want to be an example for others that they too can achieve academic success if they are determined to do so. Poverty is not an excuse for not being able to study. I am the living example.

Remembering my mother and my younger brother

There was never a day that passed by, where I missed without thinking of my demised younger brother and mother. I have quite forgotten my father because he demised when I was 15 years old and 50years has elapsed since then. The grief of not having him around comes in whenever the topic of father was discussed. It saddens me then but the sorrow does not affect me now. However whenever I recollect that my brother and mother have demised, I become depressed and sad. There have been many moments when I had shed tears for not having them around.

Whenever I had cash flow situations I cry out for my brother because he had relieved me many times before by forwarding me the required money. Similar to the story of Rama in the epic Ramayana, Letchumanan was the supportive younger brother for Rama. The role displayed by Letchumanan as a younger brother to Rama was really exemplary. My younger brother's role was quite similar to the role of Letchumanan towards me as his elder brother. He was very obedient towards me and carries whatsoever tasks I give him. He met a tragic motorcycle accident in the year 1982 when he was only 28 years old.

My brother owns a car but unfortunately on that fateful day he took the motorbike to work. He mentioned to me that his car was having some gearbox problem and the need to use his motorbike. On that particular morning I too was getting ready to attend college for some holiday programs. He left the house earlier than me but we met again at a petrol station along the Federal Highway when we stopped to pour petrol. My brother looked at me meaningfully and I waved him goodbye to acknowledge his look. It never occurred to me that would be the last communication I had with my brother.

Since he was using the motorbike lane I would not know what was transpiring at the motorbike lane because cars use different traffic lanes. I have passed by without realizing my brother was in agonizing pain when he hit the tunnel wall near the EPF (Employment Provident Fund) Building. He was rushed to the University hospital due to his head injuries. According to the hospital authorities he fell into comma on that day itself. It seems he was in great pain and the hospital had to sedate him with some pain killers. All these were narrated to us by a patient whose bed was beside his.

On that day, at night both my mother and I were complaining of him not coming home in time. My mother was worried and I assured her that he could have gone visiting to my elder brother's house and putting up a night there. As usual I went to attend my college lectures and this time I told my mother that I would not come back for the night because I wanted to stay in the college hostel. I wanted to avoid travelling from home to college since I was already provided a room to stay. The following night I was awakened by my elder brother who came by to inform me that my younger brother was admitted into the hospital due to an accident. I followed my brother to visit him at the hospital and it was pathetic to see him in a state of comma. We could do nothing for him except to offer prayers for him.

The police came looking for us to inform that he was admitted to the University hospital and my mother received the news. My neighbors helped her to locate my elder brother who then visited the hospital to locate the whereabouts of my younger brother. I stayed at the hospital to handle my brother's matter. The hospital tried to revive him but he had to succumb to the head injuries sustained from the impact of knocking the tunnel wall. His demise was tragic to my whole family. My mother was a wreck and she was very lost without him. I was afraid she would go insane because her grief was very bad. She took a long time to forget him.

I made sure that my brother's funeral arrangements went well. I informed my relatives and his friends. We had a large crowd attending his funeral mainly because of his untimely demise at a young age. There was a discussion whether to bury him or cremate him. Some were of the view that he was a bachelor and it would be appropriate to bury him. I was not keen in burial but more agreeable to have him cremated. My elder brother too agreed with me and we were the decision makers for the funeral arrangements. We had him cremated at SS 2 Cremation Grounds at Petaling Jaya.

Until today I cannot forget him and have told my children about him. My son was influenced by my story telling that he chose his career similar to my younger brother. My son is an architect and my brother was a civil engineer. He chose along the lines of his uncle. Probably my stories of his uncle must have influenced him lot. My mother too has shared her stories to my children when they were young.

I was unmarried at the time of my brother's demise. I married my wife after his demise and had to do so because mother was getting derelict, with the memory of my younger brother. The marriage did good for us because the presence of my wife at home made my household more settled. Soon with the presence of my daughter and son into the family fold made my mother to divert her sorrow. Her focus went to the grandchildren and they were her new world. The tiny tots brought cheer into the household. My wife did not know him but upon listening to my mother's stories felt that she too knew him. She reminds me every year of my brother's funeral anniversary.

Even now I go melancholic whenever I think of him. Life has to go on and my son is the living legacy of my brother. He intends to upkeep this uncles 'example of hard work and make his father proud of him by telling me that he will do well to replace the memory of my brother. He wants me to be proud of my brother by wanting to emulate him.

Sometimes I wonder whether my brother was reborn as my son. There were many similarities which both have. Both do not like milk products and certain foods. Both are left handed and both are quick tempered. They are focused in whatsoever they do. Both treat me with respect and love me dearly. Anyhow let it be, I love both of them.

My mother is my living god. In Hindu thinking there is a mention that mother is the first god, followed by father then guru (teacher) and the last is god. In whatsoever rating it was I always held her to the highest esteem. She was very endearing to me. Her demise on 29th July 1998 was the most paralyzing day for me. When I went to visit her in the morning at the hospital the news of her demise struck me like a thunder bolt. I nearly fainted and my tears were endless.

I adored her for all that she has done for me. She was the best mother for my sister, elder brother younger brother and me. Despite her lack of education, she could visualize the value for education and was a reason for me to pursue higher education relentlessly. She encouraged both me and my younger brother to study hard. Her continuous reminder that education pays has rewarded me with a permanent job as a teacher and a secured livelihood. She was also instrumental for my academic success.

Her relentless will to educate us was the ambition that was left by my father. He must have influenced my mother for her to know the value for higher education. They were loving couples. When he passed away she wanted to keep the legacy of my father to provide the best of education for us. In that pursuit she ensured that we are taken care of the expenses and she shared us the truth that she was educating me and my younger brother with a tight budget. We realized that and made sure we studied hard in order to score good marks.

Her continued guidance until the day she demised has kept me motivated to excel and do well in whatsoever I am pursuing. I have adopted her methods in encouraging others to study well by being frank to my students. I discuss with my students as to the real situation I am handling. I discuss with the students the educational issues at hand. We list out the issues and from the issues at hand I discuss with the students frankly the matters that mattered most to them. In doing so my students generally obtained good results in their examinations.

In my mother's thinking she felt that I would make a good teacher and her ambition for me was to be a teacher. Even though I was working as an accounts clerk in a reputable firm she advised me to make arrangements to become e a teacher. Due to her persistence I applied to become a teacher and got myself admitted to a teacher training college in Cheras. I learnt teacher's skills after spending two years at the teacher's training college. My experience at the college was very good and it provided me a broad scope towards knowing things.

At times I used to detest my mother's choice of the career for me. The pay was never lucrative in comparisons with other jobs. However I chose to remain being a teacher. She was only instrumental for the decision and I am the one who have accepted it. I have accepted the job's status and its glory for my own reasons. I always felt secured and the job as a teacher was relaxing. The comfort zone was too welcoming for me to remain as teacher. For 35 long years I have endured the job and on retrospect it was my destiny to be a teacher all along. Probably my mother knew that the teacher's and not other jobs were appropriate for me.

My mother chose to stay with me and her visits to my elder brother's house were short and she always insisted on coming back to my house. My younger brother, mother and I were comfortable with each other. Our lives took a sudden turn when my brother met an accident and he could not recover from the injuries. He passed away on the fateful day of 14th August 1982. The tragedy hit my mother the most and she could not accept the demise. She fell into depression and I was afraid that she would become deranged. It was then that I yielded to her requests that I be married. Looking at the situations at home, marriage was the best option I had to keep my mother occupied for the marriage preparations.

She used her network of relatives and friends to get me a wife. I relented to the practice of "match making" being practiced in our family circle. She chose a petite girl from the north with the right credentials for her standards to become my wife. However I did use the occasion to talk to my wife- to-be on the suitability of us becoming a marriage pair. She consented and upon her agreement I too agreed for the marriage. In the mirth of the marriage arrangements my mother could forget her sorrow on the loss of my brother.

Soon after marriage the family's vibrations changed. My wife brought in cheer and her tender care for my mother dissipated her sorrows and she became normal with her affairs. Time and tide slowly healed my mother from her sorrow. Her new found joys with my daughter and later my son occupied her days happily. She had many stories to share with them. My children too adored her company and they took delight when my mother bribed them with sweets and chocolates. Her childhood stories interested my children and until now they do treasure her stories. Their bonding with my mother was good.

Upon returning from school she was the first person for them to narrate their happenings'.

The presence of wife, a family unit with two adorable children and a granny made me more settled as a person. Though I was the bread winner for the family my mother still retained her leadership as the matriarch of the household. Luckily for me my wife was never a threat for her and things were rather smooth for me and family. We seldom had any quarrels and participated into family activities as one unit. We could accept my mother's role as a matriarch because we found her acceptable to our wishes and expectations. She was an advocate of the extended family concepts and she was insistence that we practice that too. Due to her wishes and requests we have good relationships with my cousins and wife's cousins. My mother was a respected matriarch in our family circles.

She was always caring for me and insisted that I should carry the family tradition of my father's legacy. Frankly there is nothing great of our ancestors but she insisted that we must hold on to the tradition of having self respect and family dignity governed. She abhorred me when I come home with alcohol smell. For her smoking and drinking liquor is a taboo. Money management was another factor that she passed on her skills to my wife. My wife learnt prudence and thriftiness from her. Her 'motto' was to never borrow and never lend money to others. We follow this practice obediently to her precepts. We have passed these traditions to our children and they have agreed to follow their granny's request.

Though my mother was an illiterate in her own terms she wanted me to pursue higher levels of education. She was instrumental for me to pursue to the Higher School Certificates, the Chartered

Secretary and Administration (ICSA -my first degree) and later Masters in Business Administration (MBA). She seemed to know that education pays and it brings in respect. Her reverence to the deity, "Saraswathy" was more forthcoming than her reverence to the deity, "Letchumy" was more pronounced. "Saraswathy" is the deity we pray for education excellence. We do have more pictures of Saraswathy at home than pictures of other deities. Probably due to this phenomenon we have many books at home. Our home environment is skewed towards studying and learning.

On 29th of July 1998, my mother took her last breath and her demise jolted our peaceful family. None of us suspected this was coming because she apparently looked healthy. She was vibrant with joy and stories. A few days prior to this she complained of high fever and medications at a regular medical clinic got her recovered.

I bought her some "roti canai" thinking it was her favorite food and she could recover better after eating it. However she complained of chest pains at the same night. I rushed her immediately to the hospital and she was warded immediately. According to the doctors she had a heart attack and was sent to the Intensive Care Unit (ICU). She recovered from it and was sent to the normal ward. In all probability she was her normal self and we least suspected that she would meet her second attack. She succumbed to the second attack and caught all of us unaware of this fateful news.

We have to accept the news and due preparations need to be made for her funeral. Her demise attracted a big crowd from our relatives, kin and kind from all over Malaysia. She was popular amongst our circles and thus a large crowd gathered to pay their last respects to her. I was remorseful and very sad because I least suspected that this could happen to her. I blamed myself for buying the 'roti canai' which had a high oil content that possibly triggered her heart attack. Until today I do not eat 'roti canai" as a self induced punishment for being the cause for my mother's early demise. Many people came forward to help me in ensuring that the funeral rights were properly emplaced and carried out. The family took the decision to cremate her and have her ashes thrown into the sea.

My respects for her doubled when many family elders called me up to remind me that my mother has not troubled us by being bed ridden. Taking care of a bed ridden elderly person could have been a burden for the family members and my mother had chosen not to bother us with that trouble. Though taking care of mother was not an issue but in retrospect it could have been a burden if she had been bed ridden. Her demise made me very sad and it took me sometime to recuperate and accept the reality of the demise situation.

Her glamour and dignity was a spectacle for me and my family. I told my children to keep her legacy going and they do not have any qualms of not wanting to adhere to this request from me. To them she was an adorable grandmother and she was a pleasant memory for them. They too attribute their educational success due to her encouragements. She had also been instrumental for their success too. They loved their grandmother.

Reflections of the past

I am now 65 years old and the environments have changed drastically. A few years ago it was apparent that there were no users of the android phones and even if they did, it was rare indeed. However practically everyone now owns an android phone and finds life difficult without one. What a transformation.

At one point of my life I did not want to acquire a hand phone with the notion that the house phone is enough to fulfill my communication purpose. With the introduction of SMS and WhatsApp messaging the androids are a must to own. Times have changed and we need them to move forward.

I could not understand why the youngsters were glued to their phones. Even at family functions the teenagers or rather the young adults' were glued to the phones. They are oblivion to the family discussions. At times I have to reprimand them to gain their attention. Everywhere and every time I am observing the change in the patterns of human behavior. Printed materials were being replaced by on line print media. The android phones have improved the technologies of telecommunications and data storage by successfully combining these two uses via the android phones.

Over the years there has been an upsurge of electronic 'devices' improvements and it is transforming the world in such huge scales. Personal desk computers that monopolized office work replaced the typewriters only a decade ago are themselves are being replaced by the lap-tops and other android devices. The world is transforming rapidly and I am a living witness for these transgress of technologies. It seems the transformations are happening as fast as within three months time wave. I am hearing of the driverless cars in the near future.

The children of the present generations are living in a luxury environment compared to our times. Their schools are mostly within a radius of about five miles only. The time taken to be in schools is made easier with the availability of school buses or parents providing the transports. Children in rural areas are however still dependent on bicycles and they ride to school on their own. Compared to the years of my childhood where I personally experienced cycling for nine miles and a bus journey of fifteen miles. I had to wake up at 4.00 a.m.in the morning and reach home after school at 4.00 pm in the late afternoon.

What a contrast with the children of the present. Secondary schools were always located at the major towns. Some schools offered school hostels for students who come from far. I was offered a school hostel only when I was in Form Four and Five. Better facilities at schools are other added features for the present day students. They are offered free school text books and need not pay school fees.

These simple facilities were not available at my time of studying. Many of my friends dropped out of school due to these factors of not being able to afford the school fees. I was one of the lucky few who could continue going to school until Form five.

When I make the comparisons with my time of schooling and the present day schooling there is a big difference. Life had changed and so would be the environments of the new world. I am however fortunate and apt to make the comments for the two differing periods of time zone. In the first instance my observations were as a student and later my observations were based as a teacher having access to more direct information.

One glaring change that has resulted over the years is the decline of the English standards. During my school days we used to have school dramas based on William Shakespeare and that was a part of fine art in schools which were missing nowadays. Schools nowadays have no time for all these non examination pursuits. Parents themselves will consider all these as waste of time and being fruitless.

Parent of my times were ignorant and were oblivion of the scopes that would be good for their children. They leave the entirety to the teachers and oblivion of what that should be best for their children. That pact made it easy for the teachers to guide their kids into areas of drama and fine arts. However parents' of nowadays are different. To many of these parents', children pursuing dramas are a waste of time. They will not allow their children to loiter and waste their time away. The game of paper chase had set in.

They are more concerned as to how many A's their children can get in the public examinations. The Standard Operating Procedure (SOP) is the numbers of A's their children get in the examinations. The schools get graded according the number of A's the school can produce in a year. Some parents even prefer their children to avoid school sports and clubs activities. The environments have changed. Instead of obtaining holistic education the children only get to pursue their academic subjects. To them they learn not to learn the subject content but only to score well. As thus these students are spoiled for academic success.

In the process of paper chase, the quality of the English language per say has dropped tremendously. To make matters worse the school system adopted the tasks of answering the questions using multiple choice methods. They shifted to this system mainly to make the tasks of marking easier. Students requiring answering their examinations in subjective mode would need thinking and expressing skills. All these qualities are not being practiced whilst in school. That explains the reason as to why the students from public universities are not fluent in their English expressions.

When I was schooling the medium of instructions was English and all subjects excepting Bahasa Kebangsaan were taught in English. The quality of the English language in Malaysia was of a high standard then. Malaysia and Singapore were known countries that possess a high level of English command. Compared to the quality of English in India, Malaysia had a good reputation where both our spoken and written English were of good standards. During our time of schooling our School Certificate papers (presently the SPM) were marked in Cambridge, London and hence there was a necessity to maintain the quality.

In addition to all these, the teachers of our times also played an important role in maintaining its quality. They were quite dedicated and hardworking educators. They went the extra mile to ensure the students are up to mark by providing personal coaching. I was fortunate to have such good teachers who were responsible for my character building. Many of my present qualities are inherited from their examples. To them I owe them tons of gratitude.

I had a teacher whose name was Mrs. Subramaniam to whom I owe my gratitude and respect until today. When I was in Form four she insisted that everyone in the class should read at least one book for one week per person. She also checked our Assignment books to ensure that we have read the book as per her instruction. We were asked to provide a simple synopsis of the content that was from the book. I remember my friends use to copy from each other and narrating in the Assignment book as though they have read.

On the contrary I followed her instructions diligently and due to her insistence I found my quality of English had improved tremendously. Her request for us to read a book each week got me glued to the habit of reading. I have never failed to comply with her request. I still dutifully read at least a book a week. For all these years since 1967 when I was in Form Four I have been reading a book a week until now. Imagine the number of books I could have read.

There were times I used to read more than one book per week and the habit of reading a book per week is still being maintained by me. I am now 65 years old and on an approximate note 50 years has elapsed. I could have at least read a minimum of 2,600 books at the rate of reading 52 books per year spanning for a period of about 50 years. Frankly I have read more books than that amount. Her influence has made me to become a well read person. Many of my friends have complemented me for this. I totally owe this gratitude to her.

Just like her there were many other teachers who were exemplary. We do owe then our respects and gratitude. In fact the progress of Malaysia should be attributed to them. They were the foundation stones for many senior Malaysians like me. It was my generation and the previous generations since Merdeka in 1957, who laid the infrastructure for this beloved country. The present generations are easy followers of the system that we have left as a legacy.

Sadly the dedications of the teachers have dipped and it would be remote if we can find any teachers who can fit in as exemplary in comparison with the old timers. Times have changed and so is the education policy. The aim of the present education is to thrive and obtain as many "A" achievers as possible. That is the mark for comparison and the school that produces more "A's" stands tall as the better school and acknowledged as an efficient institution. With the new achievements and targets, the focus has now shifted to paper chase games. Due to these factors, sports and other co-curricular activities are taking a back-sit nowadays.

Schools are not the same unlike old times. There are more amenities and more funds to spend. Just prior to public examinations students need to be in top gear. They need to listen to endless talks on the "Techniques of scoring more "A's" in each respective subject. Teachers who were experts in their respective fields were invited by the various schools to give a talk on how to score for the respective exams. These efforts have shown results and thus many students and schools follow this approach.

When the censuses were made the schools that achieved best results were highlighted. Students who scored the most "A's" are displayed as though they are the best achievers for the year. The paper chase had begun and parents ensure their children start early. They force their children to attend tuition classes as early as Standard Three. I was told that some children attend as many as three tuition classes for each subject just to ensure they get to score a "A" in that particular subject. These pursuits of the paper chase have left little time for the children to pursue or experience any childhood activities or games.

Political environment has changed over the decades. Tengku Abdul Rahman the 'Merdeka' initiator and the founder of Malaysia was a visionary leader. He wanted to ensure all Malaysians will live in harmony and progress the country peacefully. He did not want to rock the boat in replacing English with the national language by introducing Bahasa Malaysia. He had wanted to make the changes gradually but due to divisional politics and political expediency the supremacy of the Malays emerged.

National riots sparked based upon the racial tones broke up in the year 1969 and it is known famously as the "May 13 riots".

The riots brought in transformational changes into the country where Bahasa Malaysia was given prominence over the English language. The Malay political parties were emphasizing the Malay language and were insisting that the Malay language be used as the medium of instruction. Then there was the need to create an equality of the Malays to uplift them to the standards of the Chinese and other races.

The landscapes are changing and more universities are being built. More children are going to schools and more universities are being built to cater for the ever increasing number of students qualifying from the schools. During my time for higher education we had to weave our way through the higher education ladder due to shortages of space at the public universities. Competition was stiff.

The advent of NEP (New Economic Policy) changed the entry quotas giving a better priority for Bumiputra students. Many Non-Malay or Bumiputra students got left out due to lack of university places. The scramble for places for the university created a furor amongst the non Malay communities. Due to the pressure exerted by the non Malay political parties, "twinning programs" were set up by the private universities.

These Private Universities were the savior even though the fees were more expensive.

Twinning programs conducted by the private universities provided a big gateway for non Malay students to attend the programs of their choices. It reduced the tensions and frustrations of the non Malay communities who were actually deprived from their right to pursue higher education.

Despite the providence for higher education, the Non- Malay students had to pay a higher price for their education. It did hurt the pockets of the parents who wanted their children to pursue higher education. However there were also many students who could not afford had to back out and join the job market. I was a natural drop out because I chose to leave Form six very much earlier knowing my family would not be able to afford me studying further.

It was a wise of the government to open the doors for more foreign universities to operate in Malaysia. Many United Kingdom, Australian and other foreign universities opened their campus in Malaysia. These universities also attracted many students from other countries to study at these universities in Malaysia. The fact remains that it would be cheaper to study in Malaysia than in United Kingdom, Australia and elsewhere. Many foreign students are flocking to Malaysia. Malaysia is now transforming itself as a hub-place for university studies.

LimKokWing University, Taylors University, Help University, Sunway University, Monash University and some other similar universities and colleges are attracting students from the Asian region to study in Malaysia. It is even attracting students from the continent of Africa. Influx of foreign students into the private universities campuses make the status of Malaysia to go up in ranking it as a hub for tertiary education. These new demo graphs make the universities cosmopolitan.

The presence of more universities in Malaysia has quite transformed the structure of Malaysia. It now has a spectrum of more educated people with tertiary education in our midst. Some of the foreign students prefer to stay back in Malaysia. Some are already doing business with the local partners. Over the last decade Malaysia has a new face. The Malaysian outlook is changing and it is becoming vibrant again. The youths are getting interested and becoming active into politics.

There are about 33 Universities in the country which includes both the private universities and the public universities. With the advent of more universities, students could now handpick their choice for the private universities they want to study. However places at the public universities are still limited. The private universities come in handy to fill in the gaps.

The government is promoting higher education by providing a financial assistance by creating a helping arm for students to seek educational loans to pay their fees. The helping arm is the PTPTN government body. Upon graduation and getting a job they were required to pay back the amount borrowed. This scheme has helped many parents from their financial worries and it is great relief for the students.

The gateways to enter universities have changed and we have more students pursuing higher educational opportunities. Most Malaysian families have a graduate in their midst and this changes are good for the Malaysian environments. The landscape of literacy has changed the demo graph of the country. More people are educated and do have the skills of reading and writing.

It was envisioned by the politicians that the country ought to be pronounced as a developed nation by the year 2020. This is an end that can be said as near to achieve but not yet. What matters most is that Malaysia should be heading towards meritocracy and progress. Education excellence will soon come.

Malaysian Indian youth's mournful conditions

The country is progressing at good speed and it is heartening to see much progress is happening within my own lifetime. Progress has been made from many angles and the economical situations too have improved. Malaysia has grown wholesome. It has a stable political environment and it can be considered as a peaceful country unlike others in the region.

Though the country has progressed well a large portion of the Malaysian Indian youths are in dire straits. They seem lost and are with no directions. They loiter and do nothing. Some fall into the trappings of crime and easy living. According to police statistics 70 % of youths who occupy the police lock ups for various petty crimes are Malaysian Indians. This has become a social phenomena and the government is aware of this shortcoming.

The government's offering to all Malaysians are the same even though we can pin point to tell that the Bumiputeras are favored over the other races. All are provided free education from primary to secondary and that can be considered as a good respite from the government for its citizens. However some of the Malaysian Indian youths could not follow the path laid for their personal progress and has dropped out from the system.

During my time poverty was the only excuse that the Malaysian Indians had to mention as their reasons for being a drop out but not at the present scenario. With free education provided, poverty gets removed from the equation and yet many Malaysian Indian youths get dropped out. This indicates that there are other reasons causing for the new dilemma.

Long time ago I used to hear the parable, "Spare the rod and spoil the child". I used to debate myself whether the statement carries any truth in it or not. My father was a strict disciplinarian and I must admit that my academic success must partly be attributed to him. Supposing if he had not been strict with his upbringing, could I have studied? This question used to linger in me until now.

Subsequently I became an educationist and was never an advocate for harsh punishments. As a parent I have not hit my children but however had been strict with them on many occasions. My children confessed to me that they were frightened of me more than their mother. It was the fear factor that made them to study and excel in their academic pursuits. In line with this mode of thinking are the Malaysian Indian parents very far off from their children upbringing skills that their children went of course. Wonder what could be the reason for their children failing and becoming school drop outs at early stages of their developments.

On retrospect it could be the parents themselves to be blamed for not providing the right environment to their children in their growing up stages. They could be showing bad examples and having frequent quarrels in the households that the children were accustomed to these quarrels and are fed up with their disposition. As such they could be least motivated to study and pursue anything of value for themselves. I have personally visited the slums and the flats where the living conditions are in poor taste. The environments are not conducive for the school going children. The children are neglected on the part from their parents and adults in general.

These are the children who grow up without any directions in life. For them, the schools are not the right environment catering for their needs. Schools are another place where the teachers themselves ridicule them for not being clean and not proper. The children show no interest in learning and are confused as to why they are in schools. Due to their non- learning attitudes they are left behind in their studies.

In the class examinations they do not score and the teachers rebuke them for poor performance. The scolding's become viscous for them. Hatred towards the school system starts germinating from here. The children get promoted to the next class the following year and the same pattern repeats. The pattern repeats for six years at primary levels and another three years at the lower secondary levels until Form Three where they naturally fail and leave the school system.

It is a waste of nine years of their prime life pursuing something which they did not like and understand. These unfortunate children have no motivation to excel in their studies. They just become drifters. Parents of these children are aware that their children are becoming vagabonds. They could not do anything because they themselves need help.

The school system does not attempt to correct the folly because the teachers themselves are preoccupied with results and workloads. No corrective actions are made in the early stages. By the time they are in Form Three they are already in their wild paths and are out there to create mischief. They being young and in juvenile age, the police could not take any concrete steps to remedy their behaviors'. There are no right government bodies to handle this situation.

The Education Ministry should rightfully take this problem and situation to rectify these anomalies in the schools. They should know by now that the reasons for school drop outs and what are their rectifications. A special "Task Force" or an "Administration Section" can be formed to re-educate these misguided youths who need special care and motivations to come back to the correct path. After all the role and duty of this Ministry is to provide the best education for its citizens children. The Ministry needs a shake up for it to do its duty well.

It is a downward spiral for the children who see that there is no future for them. They know that they are no good and have no desire to change. They are just drifters living day to day with whatsoever that comes along. These children are the right pick for drug pushers and the criminal gangsters. They get recruited and in no time they are already on the path of crime and mischief.

The blame game begins to roll and everyone would be blaming each other. Some blame the youth themselves because they as individuals should know to fathom what is right and what is wrong. As usual they will also blame the teachers for neglecting them early and have not done the stop gap measures. Being educationist they could have taken some remedial measures. The teachers can be rightly being blamed but they however are laden with much work and many other responsibilities that it was impossible for them to rescue these children.

The school authorities should have highlighted this issue to their department heads and brought in some relief to handle these peculiar situations. Again the school heads are also tied down with their own responsibilities and that they prefer to pass this matter to the higher authorities by telling that have already done the reporting. It is easier to sweep the matter to a corner.

The society leaders are to be blamed. They are mindful of this situation and in many ways have neglected their responsibilities. Their ignorant attitude in not taking prompt action to arrest these phenomena of school dropouts has made it to grow big. They push the blame towards the ruling government itself. Everyone gets to be blamed for these discrepancies. The truth however remains that the problem is not being solved and the situation is getting worse day by day.

The politicians focus elsewhere and they ignored these pitfalls. The Malaysian Indian leaders have failed in their role as leaders for the community. Highlighting the unfair socio economic distribution of the wealth was their primary duty. These leaders who should have sounded to the authorities did not do so. At least some actions could have been taken to rectify the situation.

The individuals ought to be the responsible but that is not happening. The government could have provided the right avenues for them to rectify the situation from the beginning itself. Due to this neglect, steam had built until the Malaysian Indian community burst its banks and made ugly protest at the government. Giving rise to the movement is called as "Hindraf". The blow up of the Malaysian Indian community was instantaneous which was brewing all along. The volcano erupted in the form of "Hindraf" and only then did the government realize its folly of neglecting the minority Malaysian Indian community. The government still seems to be lackadaisical in meeting the issues at hand.

The leaders in general and particularly the Malaysian Indian leaders are taking many things for granted. They are mostly interested in other political activities rather than focusing for the public programs. Reports have surfaced that most of the Malaysian Indian leaders have not highlighted the dilemma of the Malaysian Indian youths as their representative to the respective authorities. Some NGO organizations did highlight the situation to the proper authorizes and since there were no proper instructions from the respective leaders the whole matter was swept to the corner.

Surprisingly the jobs in the country were abundant and the need to employ foreign labour became a necessity. Many youths from Bangladesh, Indonesia and other countries are here to work in the factories or business premises.

Why do the Malaysian Indian youths shy away from the many jobs that are available? The logical reason that could be attributed was that the world of crime was more rewarding than working dutifully as a factory hand. I am not implying that the youths must take up these jobs but then it could have given them responsible employment and deter them from the world of crime.

Though the 'Hindraf' was a bad publicity for the Malaysian government, a sense of eye opener had materialized for all the stake holders. The Malaysian Indians became aware that the reasons for their backwardness was due to them rather than blame all the others. The government should have realized by now that such neglect would derail the development of the country.

The community leader's realized that their attentions also need to be sacrificed for the cause and betterment of the Malaysian Indians. 'Hindraf' was truly a spark that brought in a lot of awareness to every Malaysians. Fortunately the other ethnic groups did not rebuke or were angry at the Malaysian Indian community because they knew that the anger was directed at the Malaysian Government at Putra Jaya. Infect they also rendered their sympathy and understanding for the Malaysian Indians. It triggered a sense of awareness that the Malaysian Indian community needs an awakening.

Upon this "Hindraf happening" the government quickly realized that the Indian community needs refurbishments and are taking measures to improve the well being of the Indian community. It is quite apparent that the government has created a task force to apprehend this problem for uplifting the Indian community. One such endeavor they have attempted is to spur the Indian community into small business activities. The formation of SEED under the patronage of the prime Minister himself seems to be a good initiative. The officials who have undertaken to implement the program are doing a splendid job in executing their programs.

Under the SEED programs, they have monthly gathering of about 200 Small business entrepreneurs and they are guided into the rudiments as to how to run their businesses effectively. The SEED has effectively employed the Malaysian Institute of Management (MIM) as the mentoring body for this project. Using its vast and exposed experience they were successful in garnering good speakers for the purpose. I had the opportunity to attend most of their talks and should say it has benefited most of the small business firms who have attended the talks. I am sure the small business firms should have achieved some remarkable progress by their active participation.

Besides the training programs, SEED has also made arrangements with other government agencies by arranging small business loans like 'TEKUN'. I gathered information that these 'TEKUN' loans have been very beneficial for the business people. The officials from 'TEKUN' provide guidance and auditing to ensure that they can payback their loans. This stop gap measures are helping the Malaysian Indian firms to sustain their business and improve themselves financially. It must be remembered that each Malaysian Indian Small business success will have a ripple effect on the community itself. Malaysian Indians are known for their resilience and with a little help provided their businesses will flourish and grow. The feedback is positive and more Malaysian Indians are now being usefully occupied via these small firms.

In this note it is obvious that there are more Malaysian Indian Small Medium Enterprise (SMEs) are being formed and it is a positive indication that the community are into some business activities and are being occupied usefully. The Malaysian Indians themselves know that dependence from the government will not materialize and thus it is better to have their own activities. Wealth creation is made by own efforts. This is the direction the Malaysian Indian communities are focusing now and it is the best direction for the Malaysian Indians.

Formations of many Indian based 'Non- Government Organizations (NGO)' are earmarking Indian matters and issues. They are being formed on voluntary basis and these NGO's too are forming some positive moves towards the Indian community's social improvements'.

The NGO's are also involved into activities of forwarding study loans for students who need further education. These are nurturing positive vibes and many people are coming forward to contribute for good causes. 'HINDRAF' needs to be thanked for creating the awareness. The Malaysian Indians are getting awakened. Signs of good times are coming and what is left for this community is to blend with the other communities. They should learn to thrive and survive as one Malaysian package to become responsible Malaysians.

The Malaysian Indian community only makes a composition of about 8% of the population. The demography over the years is decreasing. In the 1980's the Malaysian Indian populations stood around 12% of the population. The rate of population growth for the Malaysian Indian population is slowly declining and now it stands around 8 % only.

Factors attributing to the decline are that the most Indian families are reducing their family size by having only two or three children per household. Amongst the educated group of the Indians there is also a migration factor attributing to many small families moving over to Australia, New Zealand and Canada. Similar dilemmas are being faced by the Chinese community. They had a population share of about 42 % but they only stand to have about 25 % now. True they too are migrating away and having smaller families. The bumiputra communities on the other hand are facing an increase. The influx now stands to about 67 %. Very soon the Chinese and the Indians could be classified as minority community.

Small crime is still the monopoly of the Malaysian Indians and the government is seeking to reduce the ratios. It seems the lock ups are filled with budding Malaysian young Indian criminals. Their crimes border around petty thefts and house breaking. It seems they are now resorting towards kidnapping and collecting ransoms. Crime is a never ending game but getting involved into the crime world is contradicting the Indian culture.

Hopefully with the participation of more Malaysian Indians into business paths and with aids provided by the various NGO's to uplift the youths into education should be able arrest the growth rate in crime. These efforts could curb the crime growth and make the criminals themselves abstain from the world of crime.

The negative image of the Malaysian Indian community should reduce. The positive side of the Malaysian Indian community would rise to have more educated professionals. The transformation of the Malaysian Indian community would add pride for Malaysia.

Living the live we envision living

I have been building my life all these years. It took me many years to settle my pursuits. I have spent a considerable long time on educational pursuits. It took me three years to finish my HSC (Higher School Certificate), five and half years to finish ICSA (The institute of Chartered Secretaries and Administration), seven and half long years to finish my MBA (Master in Business Administration) and twelve years to finish my PhD (seven and half years at University Malaya where I failed on the grounds of using a wrong methodology and a further four and half years at the LimKokWing University). It took me a long twenty eight (28) years in total to be done with my paper chase for the alma mater.

This period however included my marriage, my children's birth and many other family commitments. I had to juggle between my teaching duties, family affairs and other social activtes. It indeed took me a long time to be done with my academic pursuits. Yes it indeed took such long time but the reason for highlighting here is to indicate that perseverance can get you what you aimed for. I have achieved it and I am mighty proud of it. Today I stand tall because of the PhD doctorate.

After acquiring my PhD qualifications I feel to share my innermost feelings, thoughts and apprehensions. I wanted to share because all my struggles need to be told and not to be forgotten as another passing cloud. Many senior citizens like me have a story to tell of their achievements and expectations. They have had intentions to share for the benefit of the world at large but they did not do so due to many other factors. Some could be shy and some just did not know how to go about. To some they could be ridiculed even before they begin their journey of writing.

The children are to be the biggest beneficiary and the new generation can take the cue from us to improve their lives. Basically we want the youngsters to emulate our good achievements and discard our mishaps. We prefer them to have an easier learning curve. The stories I share are similar aspirations' of many senior citizens like me. At least I am bold to pen it and express them through this book. My daughter did inspire me to write this book for her generation to benefit and overcome the turmoil's of their life. It will be a pathway for them to be strong and not to repeat the mistakes we underwent.

My personal motive is to remind the youngsters that sharing is caring. As thus the real purpose of the book is to share my journey that I underwent in life since young. It is also about coming to the fore and announce myself to the world as the new champion for the youngsters. It is about showing them the easier path and avoiding the pitfalls for their own early success. I feel it is my duty to aspire and inspire the Indian youths.

I was born into a poor family but however never really lacked anything. Though my parents' salaries as rubber tappers were low, we never had any lack for food. Being in the rubber estate my parents were resourceful to have had their own vegetable garden. We also had poultry and thus most of our food items were ever in ready supply. Items like rice, spices and other things that we could not be produced had to be bought from a retail shop. Fish and crab are bought and even that my father used to follow his friends occasionally and they caught fish. As thus there was never a lack for food.

Food was always in abundance and very seldom went hungry. Probably because I had formed good opinion and experienced good feelings about food that I rarely experienced hunger nor was there a lack for food. My mother however always kept reminding us to be prudent and thrifty. We could not spend money lavishly. Due to these early childhood factors I had always been very careful with money.

The Poverty mentality has become the very core of my being and also due to the constant reminders by my mother. Even now I dare not venture into expensive restaurants fearing for the expensive price. Lately my daughter took me to a restaurant where their charges were about three times more than the normal restaurants. I had qualms dining there because I know the amount in the bill would be rocket high. My daughter however reminded me that it was my auto- pilot into my system that has caused me the alarm. Frankly I could not enjoy the food even though it was delicious because of the auto pilot system embedded in me.

I have lately been reading many books related to "The laws of attraction". According to these laws everything operates according to our prominent thoughts. Since I held on to the thoughts of lack of money and it being my dominant thinking, lack is what that will manifest into my life. That explains as to why I always feel that there is the lack of adequacy on matters related to money. Due to this negative thinking, I have been facing money constraints always.

However after acquiring this new knowledge on the "Laws of attraction" I have attempted to change my line of thinking. I now think that there is no lack of money and things are always abundant for me. I do think and feel rich nowadays because what is that to fear when mostly I can afford things in accordance to my living style.

I have been practicing and thinking of abundance most of the times nowadays. Things are changing for me. Surprisingly I find myself with more funds than before. The reason I attest is due to the new line of thinking. I now think that I have abundance and can afford most things. I can and I am willing to spend. With this new change in my paradigm of shifting my thinking my life has changed for the better. Presently my thoughts are to be more positive than being negative.

I used to marvel, wonder and ask as to the secrets towards wealth. The rich and successful have something in common. I now have discarded the negative thoughts and only entertain positive thoughts. However due to so many years living in negativity, I have actually welcomed lack of money into my life and that has manifested. With the new paradigm shift there is more positive money flow into my life. Even though I am now a new changed positive person the 'auto pilot' in me brings me back to the negative realm.

I am earnestly making attempts to drive out the unfounded fears. I list out all the fears I am currently facing. With the guidance of simplistic thinking I earnestly convert the fears into positive vibes and am prepared to meet the worst fears on positive note. Due to this new shift in my paradigm, I shift the unfounded fears and they are wiped out instantly. It brings such good relief for all. The results are positive and my life is changing for the better. The magic part of the change is the aspect that I am willing to share.

Sometime in the 1980's, I once attended a mind changing program called "The 5 days experience" conducted by Dr. A. J. Peter in Kuala Lumpur. It was an eventful training program for me. It brought in new challenges for me. It was here that I first heard the term called "The Laws of Attraction" and saw the logics of the training sessions. I enjoyed the training session and became an ardent follower of his system

I have practiced what he preached and have found results. He gave an interesting analogy of the mind being a super computer and it can do wonders as to our commands. I have practiced his methods and found it was very relieving to solve whatsoever fears I had. When it comes to sharing there were many who did the sharing and most of the attendees have found the talk useful. It was here I became convinced that this system works. It brought in a sense of awareness that most problems are self created by ourselves and we are the ones who make it manifest them into our lives. Everyone have problems and how they go about resolving them is the crux of the matter.

It was one of the best motivational programs I have attended. Unfortunately whatever learnt I had during the time of the program was now forgotten. However this motivational program had me triggered towards self help books. I became interested in motivational topics and issues. Began using the motivational aspects with my students to motivate them and make them excel in their studies. It was one apparent good reason as to why many students like and respect me. They have told me that it was my motivational talks in the class that kept them going. In gratitude they study my subject well and attempt to get good grades. Reading motivational books was my new hobby and in the process has acquired many books for my reading purposes.

Many years passed by until a local motivator by the name, Mr. Gopalan came up with a program called "Science of Getting rich". His talk was also interesting and it appealed to me. The logics of listing all the unwanted negativity and then converting those negative thoughts to positive statements appealed good for me. In other words he wanted us to view all situations in a positive angle instead of lurking it in the eyes of negativity. The exercise of listing matters or issues in the column "Things I do not like" and then converting them as "Things I like" is a good way of making things look good on a positive note. It appealed to me. He then suggested that we convert the things we like into factors as our "Desire Statements". After simmering the things we like as things we desire he then requested us to changes them as expressions of "Allowing" the universe to fulfill these desires. I have used these logics amongst my students and have found tremendous improvements in my students' behaviors' and their outlooks.

Due to the popularity of the program and its rich contents, my group who attended the program together decided to form our own "Master Mind-Group". We called our group as BMW 14 group. The brevity represents "Best Mind Works (BMW)". Since there are 14 of us who attended the program we called it as 14 to represent the 14 members. The Master Mind group program started in 2012 and it is already five years since we began. We still meet on a monthly basis without fail. Initially we used to meet once a fortnight but due to constraints on time we changed it as monthly meetings. At the meeting we share our experiences on the LOA (Law of attraction) matters. Everyone is unanimous to continue the groupings because all of us are witnessing progress in our personal life.

Our monthly meetings are conducted professionally with the minutes reported monthly. The meetings are timed strictly covering 1 ½ hours per time for every meeting. We take turns to chair the meeting but however the secretary and the treasurer remain as constant figures for the reasons of constancy. The meetings are there to ensure that our enthusiasm does not diminish. The follow ups are essential for any motivational programs.

We are already reaping results from the continuous meet ups. Our LOA's (Law of Attraction) are working. In fact all members have shared to tell that they find parking slots are easy to come by when they need to park even at busy spots. We are experiencing more good things nowadays. Our outlooks have changed and we are more positive towards many things. We are less afraid to make mistakes and were willing to acknowledge the mistakes and move on to rectify it. We are bolder individuals now.

The new change in me is the silence factor. I now do not talk as frequently as last time. Found a new joy in silence. Trying to keep silent has made me realize that being silent provides us the strength of character. I inadvertently discovered that the less you talk the less trouble you get into. Nowadays I prefer listening rather than talking.

Noticed the silence factor brings me to a different level. Probably my mind is preoccupied with many other thoughts but realized that in due time we can tame the mind. It is possible to reduce the mind- chatter. Being silent, made me oblivion to all that is happening but at the same know what is transpiring around me. The new approach makes me feel better and less tired unlike earlier times when I do most of the talking. My family has observed me, being quiet most times and they say it is better like that. Otherwise I only confuse them with my nonsense. Being silent has its merits.

Achieving my PhD is like having my dream come true. I have achieved what I wanted to achieve and it is a great feeling to be there. Deep in my heart I know that I deserved this merit for all the hard work and time I have invested into it. I do have the pondering issue at hand as to what I should to do next. My children have given me specific instructions to stay at home. They want me to enjoy my retirement and enjoy my old age. They did not want me to jeopardize my health and get into unwanted trouble.

During these periods of quiet surrender and languishing at home when I came upon this idea of writing this book. Though it appears to be trumpeting of myself in self glory I was thinking the book can be an inspirational instrument for youths who could pick one or two insights from my book for them to seek development in their lives. I also look upon this as my contribution to the society at large and a promoter on the historical perspective of an individual. This book can be a useful tool for motivation for the present youngsters to better themselves.

Upon my resolve to write this book many things come into my mind and let this book be my tool and be the beginning to help the Malaysian Indian community in my own way. I will attempt to know their bearings and make attempts to change their lives for the better. I am being bold in doing so because I am convinced that if I can swim through my own life obstacles, others can do so too. There should be no excuse for people not to study and crawl out of their poverty.

I came to understand through my readings that the Indian Diaspora in the world are doing well except for the Malaysian Indians in Malaysia. Probably the English colonial masters have placed the migrated Indians from India into far interiors of the rubber plantations by which they could be isolated for easier control over them. The indentured laborers who worked in the interior rubber estates had little influence from the outside world.

Labour-unionism began to take shape in the 1950's and only then did the estate laborers became aware of their rights as laborers. Slowly modernity and education crept into the estate children. Every estate children were made mandatory to attend Tamil schools which were made available by the respective estate managements. Some of the children from these estates went to attend English schools. Slowly some youngsters managed to get out of the 'rut' by being educated and shifting themselves and their families into towns. That was how I made inroads to the town too.

I remember the estates could be so interior that drummers were employed by the estate management to frighten off any wild animals for the safety of the rubber plantation workers at the rubber estates. My mother narrated to me that she had to tap rubber trees near the fringes of the jungle which were the boundaries of the rubber estates. These drummers will be hitting their drums until the rubber trees around the fringes of the jungles or borders were tapped. During the later part of the mornings when the rubber tappers wanted to collect the latex, the drummers will then be around again to frighten these wild animals. I still remember vividly as a young boy, tigers had been captured by game rangers and they were paraded in the shop area of the rubber estate. That was the environments and conditions of many rubber plantations throughout West Malaysia in the early years of rubber cultivation in Malaysia.

The bulk of the estate populations were illiterate and they have been subdued by the management for far too long. The second generations of their children were still ignorant by nature but however they have became more knowledgeable than their fathers. With the advent of unionism, the tappers became bolder than before. Mobility amongst the laborers also took place via marriage and other means.

One obvious means where mobility between the rubber estates escalated was when Tamil movies made an entry into in the rubber estates. When the movies were shown in one estate there would be some kind of mobility whereby the youngsters from another estate cycled to the nearby estates in groups to view the movies.

The Malaysian Indian community in West Malaysia took some small steps towards modernity and education. Moving to towns was itself a sign of progress even though life in towns' could be more constrained. The rate for progress had been slow. Malaysian Indian parents are now aware that education does play an important role to uplift oneself. Many NGOs were formed to effect the changes for the society at large. These change movements determine the future for the Malaysian Indians in Malaysia.

My family is my new world

I must thank my friend's wife, Elizabeth for reminding me early that family is more important than friends. During my MBA days she noticed that I was a frequent organizer for meet-ups with friends. She noticed that because I frequently called her husband for the meet ups.

The real reason for our gathering was to discuss our MBA topics and we have formed a study-group to discuss our assignments. Our MBA group was planning to depart to United Kingdom for a seminar at the Durham University. It was at the airport that she chose to advice me that she felt that I was neglecting my family and yearned for the company of friends. Her advice was simple, "You neglect them now then at your old age they have every right to neglect you".

It was long twelve hours flight to London and in that space of travelling; I had time to contemplate the advice given to me by Elizabeth, a Swiss lady who married my Malaysian Bengali friend. At the same time I remembered the caricature of a cartoon strip that depicted a story of young parents sending their child to a baby sitter. The parents had no choice but to send the kid to the baby-sitter to take care of the child. Being busy at work, they had to leave the child under the care of the baby sitter. The child was wailing and crying to yearn for the company of the parents. The parents had to comfort the child that they will be back soon to take the child back after work. On the same note the cartoon depicted that after many years the parents were now old and the child has grown into a fine young man. It was now his turn to send the parents to old folks home because his work demands his focus to be at the job. Though the parents were complaining to their son that it was unfair of him to send them to the old folk's home he now comforts them by telling them he will visit them whenever time permits. The tables had turned now. On retrospect's I realized how important it was to give attention to the children and the family.

Her timely reminder was valuable and useful. I realized that during those periods I used to frequent pubs and spend a lot of time with friends on some pretexts or another as though it was useful and necessary. In truths there was never anything really important or constructive on those meet ups. During that particular flight just after my friend's wife reminder that got me into thinking and I realized that my kids and young wife would need my presence at home. Realized too that men's neglect could disrupt the family's bondage and it could be the beginning of problems. I was glad and fortunate that the advice from my friend's wife pricked my conscience.

After the seminar trip from the University of Durham and back home, a new realization has overtaken me. There is a lot of work that need to be done to score good marks for the remaining MBA assignments. Focusing and answering the various modules at Stage two, three and four of the MBA program made me realize that studying can be a joy too. I became engrossed in finishing my MBA studies. The last part needed me to finish a Dissertation paper. I chose to do a topic on "Electronic Banking"

My duties as a teacher and studies for my MBA occupied me. My family members began to see more of me at home. In due time my daughter and son became very close to me. It was a better joy to be with your own family members than out to be there with my friends. It provided me stability at home. I loved the new lifestyle and it was really joyous. Had more money left to spend for the children? Taking out the family for a dinner or a film show had provided me the appreciation to thank my friend's wife for giving me the right advice at the right time. Truly I am ever grateful to her.

My daughter and son became very close to me. They forced me to tell them stories and also insisted on giving them bed time stories. As I narrated to them the stories can see the wonder in their faces. They became interested in knowing more stories and that was how I introduced them to the world of reading. They began to like reading and soon their grades in the school improved. They became better students and ranked top in their respective classes. In addition they were also chosen to become school prefects. That gave them, responsibilities and it kept them busy.

My daughter in due time became a science stream student and was showing signs and leanings towards medicine. Since it was her passion to become a medical doctor she had to focus on her performance to obtain good grades. Good grades are necessary for admission to do medicine. She did not get admission into the public universities but she managed to gain an entry into one of the private universities. Though the fees were high, I managed to raise the funds to make her a medical doctor. Presently she is a medical officer in a Malaysian government hospital.

My son on the other hand disliked blood and the smell of medicine. He chose to become an architect due to his interest in art. Since young both my daughter and son have been attending art classes and over the years they have acquired good artist's skills. On a personal note I wanted my son to take up accountancy and follow my footsteps not as a teacher but as an accountant. He declined and on his own free-will, chose to take up architecture as his chosen field. Presently he is pursuing a Master's program at a reputable private university. The path he chose has a promising career path laid for him.

My children are now grown up and they are on their own career paths. With their absence my wife is closer to me as my companion. Her demands are little and she loves my presence at home. After finishing her household chores she loves watching the television serials and that was her favorite past time. Otherwise she loves to visit Hindu temples and will make demands to take her there.

I too however enjoy driving to the temples and make enquiries as to the history of the temples. We also enjoy partaking into the activities of the temples and most times we end up having lunch or dinner at the temples. My wife loves temple food. According to her taking temple food has medicinal values. I however have no qualms in taking the temple food when it is being offered at the right times. Taking her to temples now and then keeps us happy.

Both my wife and I are conservative and we value towards keeping the family traditions. It is our tradition that we ought to arrange marriage partners for our children. Though the time has not come for them to marry as yet, I am in a dilemma as to give my children the freedom to choose their spouses on their own or we arrange suitable marriage- partners for them. I let time and destiny do the decisions later.

With things more settled now, my family as a unit is close and cohesive in our decision makings. All four of as a family unit respect the Hindu religion. The tenets in the household revolve along the lines of Hinduism. We have gone on pilgrimages together. Our favorite temple we frequent is the "Maranthavandar Temple "in Maran, Pahang near Kuantan. This temple is dear to all of us. I have been visiting this temple since my bachelor days. I have continued visiting the temple after my marriage and with the kids since they were young.

Our directions are clear. When we are confronted with any issues we visit any of the temples to request for solutions. Sometimes we consult the priests as to his suggestions to thwart the issues at hand. We follow and mostly our problems dissipate into thin air. All of us in the family are agreed that our gods do answer our prayers. We are fortunate that our residence is near a famous temple in Klang. My house is near the Perumal Temple and we walk to the temple anytime we feel like it. Sometimes we go as a family unit and sometimes we go individually. Lord Perumal has become our next door neighbor.

With our leanings rooted in our Hindu gods we do not have any doubts about the religion. However there are frequent ambiguities arise in the practice of Hinduism. There are some temples that do practice animal sacrifice and how to accept it into my norm of the Hindu belief system. There are many other matters that do not conform to my likings but again who am I to complain or object. The best policy I follow is to avoid all these differences and be happy with my own version of understandings. In that way I do not have any quarrels with the others.

Though Hinduism in principle believes in one supreme god but it has diverse approaches. As Lord Krishna mentioned, "All paths lead to me and so are the rivers that fall into the same ocean". To my understanding all religions talk about the same god and therefore accept all paths are in praise of the same Lord. Whenever a debate arises on gods or religions I avoid taking part because it will be a futile talk. To me all of them are correct in their approaches and all are wrong holding to their way as the only way in this issue. Best I avoid.

The love for my religion enhances my love for my family. We invite other families to partake into our poojas. We also join their poojas which enable us to have more family units as a big circle of friends. It is a good way for networking because we can render help to each other. We share more people with similar beliefs and understandings and that gives us the confidence of the society we live in. When we have good friends in the midst, we do not need to look elsewhere. The family outings to the temples become good because we know we are bound to meet up with friends there. Temple going then becomes a pleasure.

I have made some small enquiries with the temple authorities and they mentioned that most of these temples survive due to these families. They sponsor various activities either individually or collectively that keep the temple active. Participation from the others is welcome and the analogy of more the merrier is always being practiced in all temples. That is why we never feel alienated when we visit a particular temple. A sense of belonging arises at all temples because the relationships are not with the people but with the main deity or deities in the temples.

It is here at the temples that I realized that the families are happier mingling with each other as temple goers. The ladies could find their own niche of people and likewise the children do find their own compatriots. Likewise the men folks are not to be neglected. They do find their own vent to become active in the temple functions. The temple then becomes a platform for community activities and various programs are put into place by which these families are willing sponsors and participants.

These activities are so vibrant and colorful that all Hindus irrespective of their main traits (some are vishnuvites and others shaivites) are united and co-operative. Sometimes cooking and servings are done together and that increases the bond ships and friendships amongst these families. Most Hindus make temple going a must for their families and that explains as one reason as to why the temples beam with devotees. It is here that my daughter got the inspiration to write her book called, "Divinity in Diversity".

My daughter's book is a depiction of her love and devotion to the various gods in the pantheon of Hinduism. She has taken the liberty to draw and paint 108 deities in her upcoming book. She then explains the roles and the purpose of that particular divinity in her book. Her purpose is to render the message that Divinity is one and she also portrays the divinity in diverse roles. Her book will be an interesting read for people from the Hindu faith. People from other faiths too can read to know more about our Hindu gods.

Her book explains the diversity through her colorful hand drawn art works and beautiful paintings. The book is yet to be published. When it is printed it could reach out to many Hindus and it explains well the diversity of the divinity.

My daughter since young was fed with the various puranic stories and the Hindu mythologies. Her interests in our gods made her to research and compile the information to illustrate the various deities. However our temple going activity as a family unit that gave her the inspiration to write and provide the illustrations for her book, "Divinity in Diversity"

My directions towards spiritual paths

My exposure in many spiritual and religious discourses has made me interested into the Hindu religion. There is a link between god and higher thinking. I cannot fathom any higher thinking without the presence of god in it.

After watching a famous English movie, "The Poseidon" that tells a story of a luxury cruise was being over turned by a gigantic tidal wave, and the struggle of its passengers to reach the top to be rescued. The film brings the message that god is the ultimate. In that film the hero was portrayed as an atheist who believed in himself and not god. He was leading a group of stranded passengers from an overturned ship to reach the top for safety. He does his utmost best in his ability to lead the people but becomes frustrated in his trials and tribulations to save his people. Finally as a last resort he shouts for help from god and seeks his clemency to save the people. The film made me realize that eventually only god is the last hope. Though it was only a film but its message was clear for me.

There are many spectacles and stories that I have witnessed and have heard that confirms the existence of god. I have no doubts about it. When I was young I used to subscribe to a free bible correspondence course. The course contents were interesting and I used to score high marks when the scripts were returned marked. It was here that I grew to be fond of Jesus and his preaching. Even now Jesus holds a special place in my heart. I have attended many church sermons and always find Christianity a loving religion.

Amongst my teacher friends I too have some friends who are from the Islamic faith. When I am in close contact with them I enjoyed their company. We do have mutual respects for each other. They are good friends with me and did find their views as not radical. Islam has been portrayed as radical by the media. In my limited understanding, I respect all religious paths. I am convinced that all paths lead to the same god.

The world is a mystery and a wonder. When we delve into it we cannot find an exact answer to it. My believe in god seems to provide some answers to our numerous ambiguities. Surrender to his marvels and greatness provides all the answers for all happenings. There is something higher and greater than us. Let me call it god. I produce here, a prayer which represents my views:

A PRAYER

Oh god, I see you in many forms
Both with forms and being without forms
In the name of all great religions that abound
With great teachings and preaching for me to follow

In humility I accept your sermons
For you have only one purpose
To have me as your child
And pamper me to your path

To both non believers and believers you show sympathy
And magnanimous is your forgiveness for all
In providing me the freedom
To make my own paths to reach you

Though I am small and weak
Will always want to seek you
For the path to make me strong
With the wisdom to know your real beauty

I seek to fight my greatest enemy – myself
Overcome all my confusions and total surrender
And be ever ready to meet you
With no shame of guilt left in me.

Apparow Sannasai PhD

Malaysia is a harmonious country where all citizens are free to practice their faith and worships. Unnecessary ugly feuds on the various faiths have not happened as yet. In Klang where I stay, we can find an Indian Muslim mosque; an Indian temple, a

Guduwara (a Sikh temple) and two churches are nearby to each other. These types of examples are all over Malaysia. Malaysia is known as a harmonious nation on these aspects. There is much tolerance and understandings from the various different faiths.

There is no disruption to personal beliefs and practices. However Islam has got special place and it is entrenched in the constitution that it is the official religion and that other faiths are free to practice their own religions. Malaysia is the best place to live and practice one's religion. Religious harmony is truly being practiced in Malaysia. Everyone accept moderate paths.

I being a Hindu have got myself joining many "Bhakti" involvements. Bhakti basically means service to god and have got into many temples activities to serve god by indulging into activities that evolve around serving the deity or deities of the temples.

When the Hare Krishna Consciousness' Movement made its entry into Malaysia, I was one of the early participants to enroll myself as a member into this movement. I admire their slogan, "simple living and high thinking". Their preaching of four precepts is good. They advocate: 1) No meat eating, 2) No illicit sex, 3) No intoxications and 4) No gambling. Whenever one can follow these precepts their life can become sublime and harmonious. They also encourage chanting of the Maha Mantra: Hare Krishna Hare Krishna, Krishna Krishna, Hare Hare, Hare Rama Hare Rama, Rama Rama, Hare Hare.

Chanting the Maha mantra can create a wonderful inner feeling. According to a swamiji from the Krishna Conscious society who mentioned that as we recite the maha mantra our past sins get wiped off slowly. He further explained, it is like removing the dust particles of our past karmas. As we go on removing the past karmas our lives become clear and we encounter lesser and lesser problems in our daily lives. I followed this path for some time but due to lack of discipline and own incapacity I could not follow all of their precepts. If anyone can follow their laid path, I am sure they can find real solace from god himself. Some of these Hare Krishna followers have a glow over their heads. Many westerners are adapting to this way of live.

After sometime I came across another movement called the "Transcendal Meditation Movement". The headquarters was in Petaling Jaya and they offered a meditation course program for 5 days. The prices are determined by us and we pay according to our affordability. A group was formed and we began the program. I really liked their techniques and it was so easy to follow. I was enthusiastic in practicing and even now I do still practice the techniques now and then.

I came to do understand that all manifestations in over lives are due to our own doings. The guru for this movement was Sri Mahesh Yogi and he had a vast following from all over the world. We have a lot of westerners' practicing this type of mediation. There is no mention of god except that we are encouraged to meditate twice in a day. They strongly advocate a meditation session in the morning one time and another meditation session in the evening. Their focus is to eliminate stress and via their meditation practice one can reduce the stress levels. Every time when I am stressed up I practice the meditation techniques to remove the stress that has been added in by me.

I know of some specific people who practice TM Meditation and have overcome their physical ailments. They reason that all health problems originate from stress and thus they feel that "stress" needs to be eliminated at all costs. I am fortunate to learn these techniques of reducing stress.

As though the above is not enough I came across astrology by default rather than by purpose. I saw a paper advertisement that Vedic Astrology was being thought in English. I became excited and enrolled to join the class. I was surprised that there were many working professionals in the class. Some of them were experienced lawyers, managers, doctors and businessmen. We had both the Chinese and Indians attending the class and all are educated in English. The tutor or rather the guru himself was a PhD man and his command of the English language was of above par excellence. He has an intricate knowledge on astrology and he was a good teacher. His explanations made me learn and understand the principles of astrology fast. Since then I have become an astrology enthusiast. I joined the Malaysian Astrological Society as a life member.

Even now I subscribe to two astrological journals and keep myself updated with the latest astrological happenings. I am well informed about the planetary movements and I know of the planet's position in the zodiac. I know how to make predictions and do so only for family members and some close friends. I do not predict for others and when I am approached I decline them politely.

There is truth in astrology but it is always the interpretations that go wrong. Some astrological practiners are half baked fellows whose knowledge does not suffice to predict correctly. It is these astrologers who are misleading the general public when they seek their advice. As thus dependence on their predictions are in question. I always suggest to my people to have two or three readings from different astrologers' to make a conclusive decision. Better still one makes use of their own common sense to make their decisions. The use of astrology is allowed in Hinduism as a guide only.

There is a saying in Hinduism that when a student is ready for a new knowledge a guru will appear for the pupil. Likewise I was yearning to know the contents of the Bhagwad Gita when I came across a learned economics professor who was willing to share his knowledge on Bhagwad Gita. He was lecturing at a reputed university and he was helping me for my PhD program at the University Of Malaya.

He is the brother in law of a close teacher friend of mine. In fact I know him when he was in school. I approached him for guidance and to help me with the analysis of my PhD thesis. It was here that I realized that he had a profound understanding of the Bhagwad Gita. He was keen to impart this divine knowledge if I can find him a group who could be interested in knowing. Very quickly I managed to gather a small group of retirees who were very keen to know more of the Bhagwad Gita.

Bhagwad Gita has much to offer us with the practical knowledge of knowing how to distinguish between duty and non duty. It gave a profound effect on me by learning to know that detachments can be a way out from misery. It is here that I learnt that all souls who have manifested as human beings are here for their own learning. It is here that I learned that our primary duty is to be focused on the specific duty to find liberation from rebirth (moksha). Birth and death are a part of the soul's journey. Our journey is a part of "maya (illusion)" and thus we need not build much apprehension in our lives. Our destination is towards achieving "Moksha" or liberation and that should be our focus.

A calling to make a pilgrimage to Sabari Hills to see Lord Ayyappa came along. A group of my teacher friends were planning to go there when invited by their friend. Since it was school holidays and I have a good company I agreed to go. My family too wanted me to go. The "Ayyappa Movement" was becoming popular and my brother- in- law who has been there was strongly advocating that I go and see Lord Ayyappa myself.

A few protocols need to be followed by all Ayyappa devotees. We must be vegetarians for 48 days and refrain from any sexual activities. Must bathe two times a day and sleep on the floor. The prayer hall in the house needs to have a picture of Lord Ayyappa and keep a ghee lamp lighted 24 hours for the whole duration of 48 days. Devotees are expected to hold house poojas and invite the 'Samis' (other devotees) to their houses when they conduct house bhajans. Charity is encouraged and providing food "anathanam" is one of them.

During these periods of 48 days my wife made sure that I practice devotedly. To give me support my whole family chose to become vegetarians and they too followed me in my trips to other devotee's houses for their house bhajans. We all became engrossed into Lord Ayyappa prayers. We all realized that this provided us the impetus to learn what is a real devotion is like. In this period of 48 days we began to love Lord Ayyappa dearly. We loved him as though he is another member of the family. It was a religious joy during this period.

I made another two trips to see Lord Ayyappa whose temple is up on Sabari Hill, Kerala, India. Followed the same group and I still maintain my fellowship with them. In the second trip my son followed me and he was a big help in getting me to climb the hill. The third trip too was fruitful and the young "Samis" in my group were equally helpful. Going up and seeing the icon of Ayyappa is like seeing himself. He acknowledged my pilgrimage to him.

It appears to be my destiny path that I have to be religious. I am now lured to be a committee member of the Annapurna Devi temple. My job is to help in raising charity funds to build the temple at the fringes of the Klang town. Half an acre of land was allocated to build the temple and the idea was mooted to build a temple for Annapurna Devi. There is no temple dedicated to this goddess and that this temple must be different from the other temples. The temple would be providing free food for all devotees who throng the temple at all times.

This temple would be conducting yoga classes, astrological classes, religious classes and other related topics. To cope with this activities' an additional building of five storey height would be erected. Hostel facilities are to be provided devotees who throng the temple for its activities.

In the beginning I was quite reluctant to join the Annapurna temple committee because it could involve a lot of work and time mobilizing these activities. However on second thought my charitable nature took over my conscience in the sense as to, why not I provide my knowledge to render my services to help the temple to raise the funds. Charity is the hall mark for the Annapurna goddess.

The temple committee was gloomy with the fear that it won't be able to raise the needed funds to build the temple. I prepared a simple working plan and showed them as to how we could raise the monies. After hearing my plan they became excited again. I told the temple committee that we can achieve our targets if we can get the help of the youngsters. Quite immediately we have about 50 youths who are willing to work to get the grace of Annapurna Devi.

Invoking the grace of Annapurna Devi will be our first priority because she is the deity for giving free food for the poor. Preaching charity will be the focus to establish the returns for the needed money to come. The donation drive can begin with Annam (food). Annapurna Devi's blessings can make it happen.

To a destiny path unknown.—spiritual pursuits

I love god and I am convinced that there is god. I have no doubts about it. With my convictions on the existence of god my life is now more focused. I do activities that are linked to my prominent thoughts. Love for god is a prominent thought and therefore my activities are linked towards activities that circle around god. I feel better and happy. That is my message and it is a free world. Everyone ought to be free to choose their life the way they want.

There is a god who is governing all our activities and it for these reasons there are many temples, churches and mosques abound in the country. This indicates that Malaysians are god loving people and their primary priority is towards the worship of their god. When the people are religious it is good for the country's administration. The people's leanings towards religion do make them as good people. It will be easier to govern good people and it explains for the political stability in Malaysia.

Though my reliance is in god, I still wonder as to how my future would be. It will be a pleasure to adhere to religious activities and be usefully occupied. I have made some conclusions. Life has to be enjoyed and cherished every moment in one's lives. The saying 'Living moment to moment' is a good catch phrase to follow. Over the years the years of living with my personal experiences, exposure and learning I have made some conclusions as to the way my life has shaped.

The untimely demise of my younger brother shook my world of reality. Had so many plans laid for him but when he passed away it took me to a sense of awareness that we are only residing in a temporary world. Nothing is certain and only change is certain. Life has to go on and we know for certain that we do not know what is in store for us. We can plan, we can manipulate and we can even dream but can never predict with certainty the exact future. Anything can happen to us in the future but however we can have plans to keep ourselves protected from any eventualities.

Since we are living in a temporary world it is better to keep our cheer and learn to be happy always. Though we cannot avoid sorrow sometimes we must attempt to bring back the cheer into us. A happy person is in a better situation to do things. I have made the resolution to make good and make myself cheerful at all times. I know sorrow and pain cannot last. Cheer and happiness can fill in the gap.

I currently read two very inspiring books that quite changed my perceptions towards life. The book by Vikas Malkani entitled "Yoga for Wealth" and "Zero Limits" by Dr. Joe Vitale made an impression into my life that I can view life from this perspective.

In "Yoga for Wealth" Vikas Malkani mentions that all us are born rich. We are endowed with abundance and it is the purpose of Mother Nature and God. However over the years of living or even possibly due to "many rebirths" our DNA has got infiltrated with so many negative vibes that we have quite forgotten or even aware that we ought to be rich with abundance. He mentions that we have forgotten that we have the trait to be rich. In his book he reveals that great gurus and seers have realized this sublime truth and they practiced richness in reality and therefore their lives are always in abundance. They do not worry unlike us. For them food and shelter is never their concern. In reality they are rich.

He mentions that this forgotten awareness is "Turiya". He explains that "Turiya" is the unseen principle that we have the richness embedded into us and we are not aware of it. He further mentions that we are living with limited beliefs and that is the reason for us being poor in wealth. It is these limitations that are limiting our lives.

He cites examples that we should live as though a pail of water from the abundant sea will not really empty the sea. He encourages us to throw away the limiting beliefs and learn to live in the principle of "Turiya" and that is live as though we are already rich. He also mentioned that it is difficult to accept this "Turiya" principle but with willful purpose, intentions, affirmations and changing the thoughts to belief that we are already rich will slowly and surely bring about the change we so desire. He cautioned that this could take time but it is worth the try.

The book by Dr. Joe Vitale, "Zero Limits" explains the lifestyles of ancient Hawaiians. In this book he reveals that our lives are dominated by two factors. One factor is "Memories" and another factor is "Inspirations". He mentions that "Memories" are the factors or events that are replaying from previous actions. Previous actions could also refer to past lives and that the actions are being replayed but in different dimensions. As thus all that is happening to us either good or bad happenings are due to past actions that are being replayed now.

It is an ancient Hawaiian belief that all are connected and that all happenings around us is due to our previous deeds. To them it is the past "Memories" that is replaying itself in the present moment. They however offered a solution to stop the bad from repeating. The Hawaiians' believed offering forgiveness' and gratitude to the past should suffice.

Dr. Joe Vitale has modified the prayers of offering into four simple statements:

> I love you
> I am sorry
> Please forgive me
> Thank you

Dr. Joe Vitale suggests that we repeat the above four statements towards the matter or person who is the source of the trouble. According to him over time the problem will cease to exist because you have asked for forgiveness and have shown your gratefulness.

This is a kind of ancestor appeasement but the book does not mention anything about ancestors. The book further clarifies that all happenings are due to the "Memories" being replayed continuously and that the only way to stop the repetitions is by uttering the four statements mentioned by him. It is like rubbing or erasing the memories and thus the memories get faded and their manifestations will become weak. With fewer memories disturbing one's journey, a person can be happy with a joyful life. This process is called the "Ho'opono'opono" The second aspect of the Hawaiian belief is the "Inspirations" and he mentions that "Inspirations" refers to new thinking and new inputs. These new inputs and aspects are from the divine.

Dr. Joe Vitale further illustrates that nothing exists at "Zero Limits", no problems including the need for intention. He emphasizes that all problems arise from memories and as thus we require "Divinity" to erase these memories. He mentions that these, 'two laws' dictate our experiences: Inspiration (Brand New) from Divinity and Memory stored in the Subconscious Mind (Old Brand). He explains that "Zero" is the rightful residence for us and Divinity, where wealth, health and peace flow, is our birthright

I am now practicing "Ho'oponopono" most of the times and have experienced great transformations within me. It has done good and it is still doing good for me. I have requested my family members also to practice and they too mentioned to me that it is working for them. Requesting for forgiveness' and showing gratefulness has now become second nature for me now. I realize these statements have brought in new meanings into my life. My acquaintances' has reported to me that they find my company with them as very pleasant. They also revealed that they find me as very accommodating to them. They enjoy my company unlike earlier days, I could have been grumpier.

The "Turiya" principle is taking its time to seep into me but however I must admit that the monetary situation of my individual self has improved. I feel rich even though my lifestyle has not changed much. I am beginning to belief that I would be endowed with riches soon. I would prefer to share this new found wealth to charity. I am making baby steps to provide "charity". Giving charity can make an individual happy and giving for a good cause is a worthwhile effort. Abundance is to be shared and thus charity will be my new pursuit.

In pursuit for wealth, health cannot be ignored. Health should be given prominence over wealth because without health, wealth does not serve its purpose. The principles of prioritizing wisdom, health, wealth and happiness are a correct path. With all my duties done I am now going to focus on health, wealth and happiness. Every other thing will follow suit on its own. As for my religious path I have decided to follow the prescribed Hindu path.

I have no quarrels with other faiths. I have good friends from other faiths and still meet them frequently. Malaysian is a country that exemplifies as a model nation that could thrive in the environment of multi-ethnic races and diversity of religions. Malaysians in general do have friends from the other races or religions. Fostering unity and friendship is a duty for all peace loving Malaysians.

I strongly believe that positive thoughts are very important ingredients to achieve success. Positive thoughts will spiral the individual to a path for continued success whilst negative thoughts will spiral the individual to a downward path. Good positive thoughts will provide a sense of good feelings which will motivate the individual to take action. The action is to fulfill the good feelings and the process will surely achieve good results. I believe good positive thoughts are the main reasons for an individual to achieve success otherwise it is impossible for him or her to achieve the goal.

Thoughts are like the seeds that we have planted some time ago and it is bearing its fruits now. A mango seed would only bear a mango fruit and not otherwise. Let us plant the seeds for success and let it achieve the fruits of success after giving some time for the germination of the tree.

It is good to dream big and dream high. It gives a sense of elation and greatness. The feeling will be good and positive. However to achieve the result one has to focus on the issue at hand. Dreaming big, focusing on the task and having positive feelings can bring about good results. The achievements could be obtained by aligning the dreams, the focus and the feelings. My focus on my studies was long but it still brought in success for me because I had a dream and it was a great feeling to obtain my PhD doctorate. More concerted focus in efforts will bring in faster results.

In whatsoever activities we are involved, we must have the end result in mind and with proper aligned focus the job of the activity will be done with ease. With proper focus and emotional stability the end result will turn to become a good expected success. We must not have any doubts on the results because doubts are like welcoming negative energy into the work field. This negativity will give rise to cause the disruption of the expected results. It gives rise to results that are sometimes favorable and sometimes unfavorable. My advice, do not have any doubt.

I have chosen to believe in god and follow the Hindu faith. I am intending to be a charitable person with the belief that I am a rich individual. I love life. I am living a life of happiness being healthy and wealthy. I am a positive individual with charity at heart and abundance thinking.

A word of advice

I believe in the ripple effect. When we throw a small pebble at a calm pond we can realize the expansion of the pond that begins from small ripples to big ripples. This is the effect I want to envision in my world. The ripples will indicate me first, family next, neighborhood, community, area, township, state, nation, world and followed by the universe at large.

Dr. Joe Vitale indicated in his book that all activities and people are connected. The above ripple effect also indicates the same thing. The whole world is made of collective actions of everyone. Everything has an effect on all things. The world we live in is a collective world.

Confucius was a great Chinese sage and his teachings are still applicable today. One of his great teachings that is still applied are his preaching's on the family fold. He mentioned that a good family will make a good community and a good community will make a great state and good state will make a great country. He emphasized on family values. Likewise we have a duty towards our family, our community, our race, our religion, our state and to our country. We can make Malaysia a great nation when we care for our family values. It is as simple as that.

History is a subject that is losing its grip in the school education system. History teaches us how the great leaders on the yonder past have ruled their countries. It will do good for the nation to adopt the strategies being used by them. We need not repeat the mistakes done by the past leaders. Our learning curve is simpler when we adopt the lessons imparted by history. However history has lost its grip and many youngsters do not like history. As a Malaysian citizen one has to know their history and they can follow the paths shown by our past greats.

Never have bad friends with you. The moment you realize that bad friends are influencing you into the wrong path, you quickly terminate their friendship. Negative friends will be detrimental to you on all aspects. They will pull you down from progressing. You do not owe them a living and they can never be a good friend for you. A good friend is the one who cares for your personal success. Again bad friends will influence you to have negative thoughts and that negative thoughts will spiral you to the downward paths. Friends who are curtailing your progress need to be cut. You do not deserve their friendships unless they are sincere in progressing along with you.

On this matter I would like to share a personal story. During my youthful days I used to frequent pubs for some drinking sessions with my friends. I enjoyed the outings and the jokes that were circulating amongst the pub goers. The outings were getting more frequent and the drinking budget expense was going above my apportioned quota, I decided to called it quits or reduce my outings.

However in the midst of these friends, there are some who insist on me following them? They even come to the house to fetch me. When they do so it is difficult to refuse them. I occasionally obliged them but then it was at the expense of my own money and time. I made a decision to stop pub going because I had enrolled to do my ICSA (Institute of Chartered Secretaries and Administrators) program. I could not afford both the time and the money. In order to avoid my friends from coming to fetch me I used to hide my motorbike behind the house. My friends seeing that there is no motor bike assumed that I have gone out and was not at home. On retrospect I believe I have made a wise decision. I am glad that I have given importance to myself than my friends. At least I could achieve my doctorate by avoiding the pub- path. It is important and necessary that we cut from negative activities and negative friends.

I always advise others to choose their friends wisely. I advise them to cut of friends who are pulling down their progress. There is no necessity to have friends who are retarding one's progress. It is a joy to be successful. Success begets success. Only when we are successful, we will have a happy family and a happy environment. Success is defined in many ways. I define success as having completed a particular task or tasks as the yardstick that can used to measure the rate of success. Monetary gains are not everything.

In the astrological zodiac chart the eleventh house is assigned to friendship and it is also the house for gains. Friends can become our detriment when we fail to choose them diligently. All those people who hinder our progress should be placed into the sixth house which is the house of enmity. Friends who do not support our progress are in reality our hidden enemies. The following describe the types of friends we should welcome into our lives:

Friendship

We all need friends
Be they good or bad
The good will remain as friends
And the bad will cease to be friends anymore.

The good friend will be your ladder for success
They will attribute you to rise and rise
For pinnacle of success belongs to both you and him
As you rise he can follow

Friends who deter you from progress
Are not your friends at all
They will pull you down and not push you up
It is best we cut them off

There are friends who on the quiet are your real enemies
They do not want you to progress
They want you to stay where they are
Friends that don't help you climb will want you to crawl.

The less you associate with these friends in veil,
The more your life will improve.
When you tolerate the mediocrity in them,
It will impede your progress.

Negative thinking and negative friends you must cut
For they will only impart negativity,
You must rise up and go above them
And never let these negative friends bring you down.

There are friends who will choke your vision
And stop your dreams
They do not increase your being
But will decrease you when you allow them to do so

Do not divulge your new ideas
To friends who are in disguise
Who is ever ready to retard you?
And drown you with their own fears.

Pick your friends who will lend you support
Support you to soar your heights
A true fact of life is that you will become like those person
You closely associate for the good and the bad.

When we are prosperous everyone wants to be our friends
Do not be beguiled for they can be temporary
A true friend will always be beside you
whether it be a good or a bad time
He will be friend indeed.

Friendship must be there to help you achieve excellence,
It s a mutual affair where together
Strive for excellence in all matters
And it is the relationship of friendship that moves the attitude

However whatsoever friendship it may be
Be they many or few
Do love, appreciate and be thankful for your family
Because they will always be your friend no matter what.

Apparow Sannasai

The above narration explains as to how one ought to have relationships with friends. When the friends are retarding the individual's progress these negatives are to be dropped off. We are nature bound wanting to be successful. Any aspects that are detrimental to his progress would only hinder one's progress in life. However there will be some good friends in our midst. They are the ones who will stand by when we are in dire need of them. A good friend is a friend who is there at the time of a need is a good friend indeed. With good friends around the corner we can conquer the world.

Successes in all aspects of life are essential to have a worthwhile and a meaningful life. The way we face life will determine the path we are envisioning and pursuit of happiness is a positive way to ensure success. Success is a measure of achievement and the measurement is determined by individuals in different dimensions.

Being a good citizen of one's country is an essential requisite for a successful person. It is the duty of every one to contribute towards the welfare of the country in any way they can do so. The country is nothing without its citizens. The country's destiny is determined by the composition of its citizens. When the majority of the citizens are living in joy and with thoughts of abundance the country will prosper. When the citizens are positive, the country will spiral towards progress and development. Abundance will drop into the lap of the country. Wealth will pave the way for better infrastructures' and stability for the nation. Joy will unfold for the people in the country.

At the end of the day we ought to ask ourselves what is the legacy we leave behind. How do our family members view us? How do our friends, relatives and neighbors view us? In the end have we been a useful citizen. Being a joyful and a good person should be the trademark we leave as our legacy. A rubber tapper's son has risen from the woods. He has made his mark as a successful person should be the story I leave behind.

End

Printed in the United States
By Bookmasters